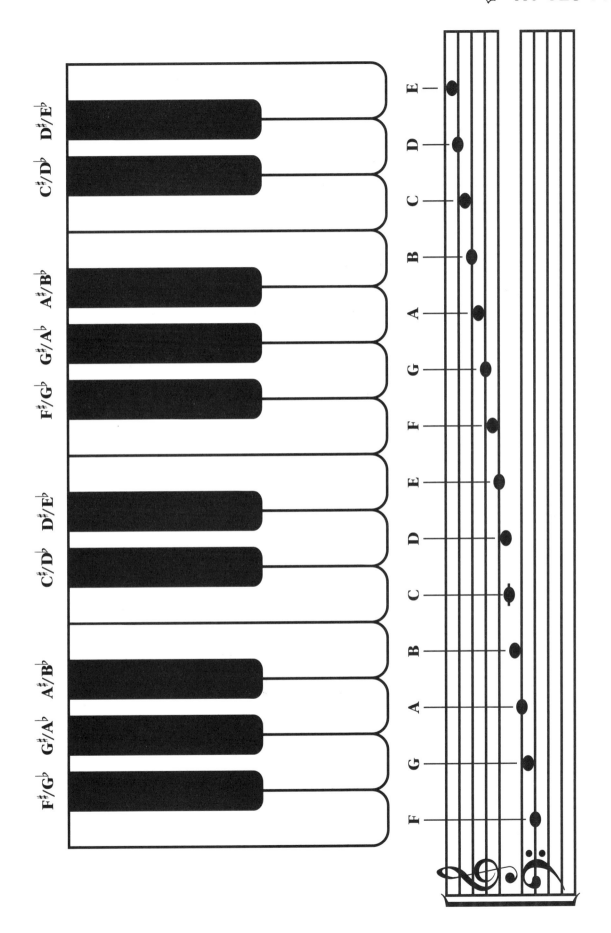

T-E
Nu-Sc39
Si-3

Silver Burdett MAKING MUSIC

Program Authors

Jane Beethoven
Susan Brumfield
Patricia Shehan Campbell
David N. Connors
Robert A. Duke
Judith A. Jellison

Rita Klinger
Rochelle Mann
Hunter C. March
Nan L. McDonald
Marvelene C. Moore
Mary Palmer
Konnie Saliba

Will Schmid
Carol Scott-Kassner
Mary E. Shamrock
Sandra L. Stauffer
Judith Thomas
Jill Trinka

Recording Producers

Rick Baitz
Rick Bassett
Joseph Joubert
Bryan Louiselle

Tom Moore
J. Douglas Pummill
Michael Rafter
Buryl Red, EXECUTIVE PRODUCER

Buddy Skipper
Robert Spivak
Jeanine Tesori
Linda Twine

Scott Foresman

Editorial Offices: Parsippany, New Jersey • Glenview, Illinois • New York, New York
Sales Offices: Parsippany, New Jersey • Duluth, Georgia • Glenview, Illinois
Carrollton, Texas • Ontario, California

ISBN: 0-382-34347-6

Contents
Steps to Making Music

Unit 1 — Let the Music Begin! — 2

Unit 2 — Exploring Music — 40

Unit 3   Learning the Language of Music   78

Unit 4   Building Our Musical Skills   116

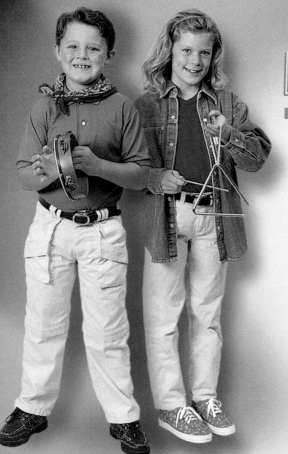

Paths to Making Music

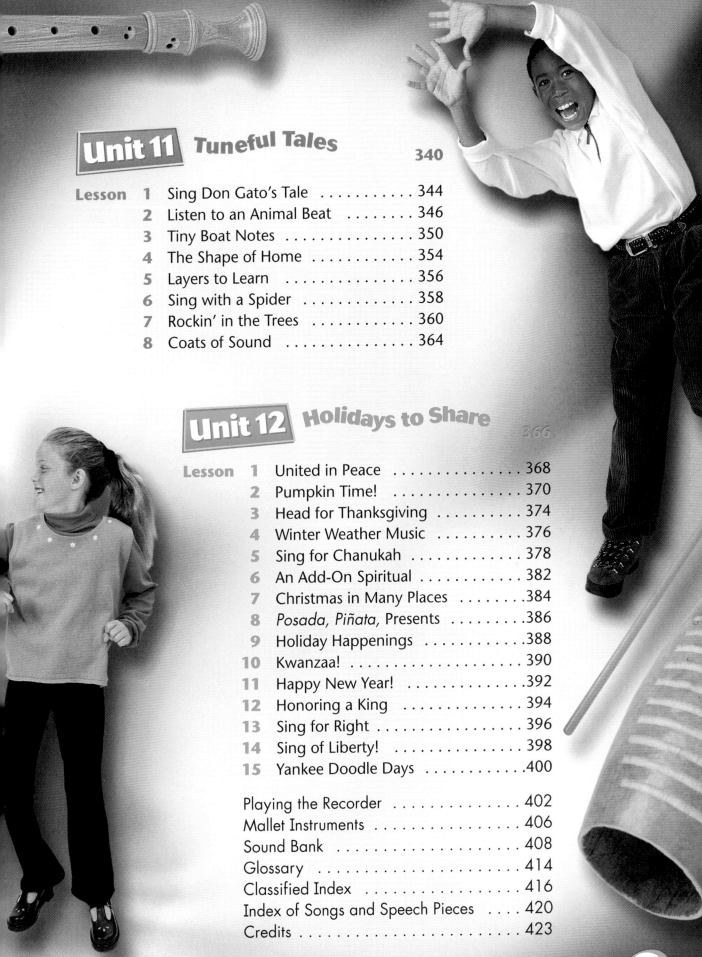

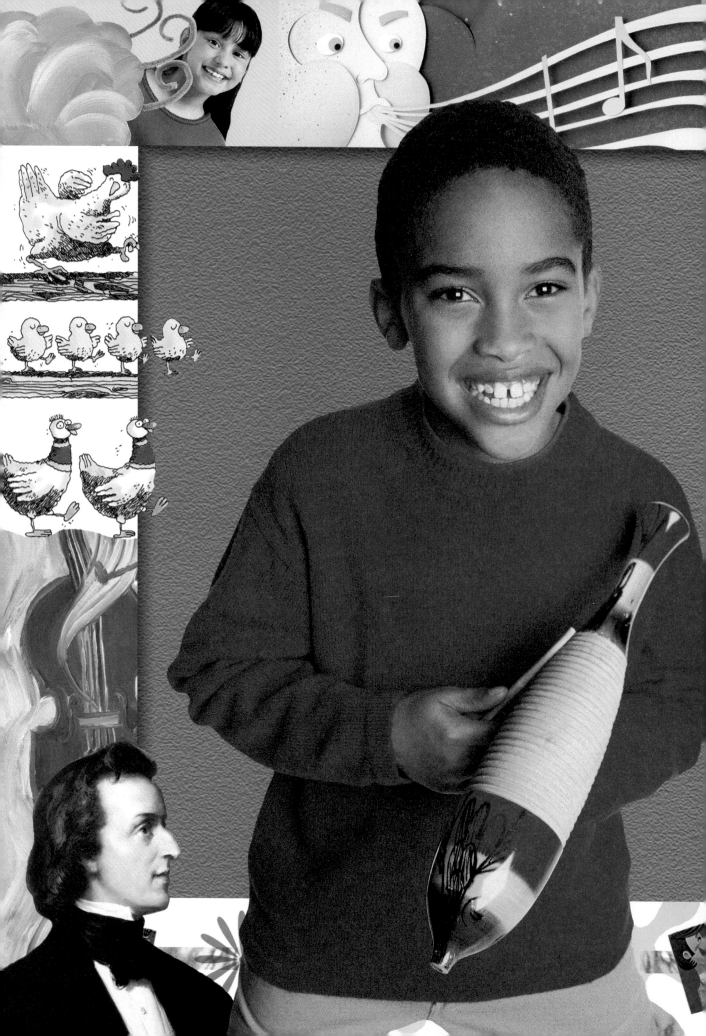

STEPS TO MAKING MUSIC

How to Say Hello

Did you feel shy on your first day of school? Did you meet old friends from last year? Sometimes it's hard to say hello to people you haven't met. Making music is a way to find new friends as you play together.

Read this poem and imagine how you can say hello to people who may become new friends.

Hello to the World
by Susan Katz

The sunshine sings HELLO
each morning as it greets the sky.
And wherever we happen to be
in the world, we smile
as each ray makes its way
in a golden HELLO
through our window.

Sing HELLO to the millions of children
who are dreaming of someone like you.
They hope to hear your HELLO in their ears
so their worlds can become united as one
with your world, and the loving embrace
of your friendly HELLO will be worn
by the world like a smile on a face.

Poetry in Motion

Create an eight-beat pattern by patting your legs and brushing your hands together. **Perform** your pattern between the stanzas of the poem.

Let the Music Begin!

How to Say Hello

Children all over the world have a lot in common. They play games and sing songs. **Listen** to this song to hear greetings in nine languages! Then you can **sing** along.

1-1

Hello to All the Children of the World

Words by Nancy Klein

Music by Nancy Klein and Pam Beall

REFRAIN

do—

Hel - lo, *Bon-jour, Bue-nos dí - as,* G' - day, *Gu-ten Tag, Kon-ni-chi wa.*

Ciao, Sha-lom, Do-brey dy - en, Hel - lo to all the child-ren of the world!

Fine

VERSE

1. We live in dif - f'rent plac - es from all a - round the world.
2. There's child - ren in the des - erts, and child - ren in the towns

G₇   C

We speak in man - y dif - f'rent ways. —
And child - ren who live by the sea. —

F   C

Though some things might be dif - f'rent, we're child - ren just the same,
If we could meet each oth - er to run and sing and play,

D. C. al Fine

G₇   C

And we all like to sing and play.
Then what good friends we all could be.

Dynamic

Move to show the **dynamics** in the song. Bounce your heels to the beat as you do each of these movements.

The louds and softs in music are called **dynamics**.

p

mp

mf

f

Watch the Signs

Look for the signs in the music that tell you when to sing loudly and when to sing softly. The signs are called dynamic marks. What do you think *mf* and *mp* mean?

p = *piano* = soft

f = *forte* = loud

1-3

Supercalifragilisticexpialidocious

Words and Music by Richard M. Sherman and Robert B. Sherman

p Sup - er - cal - i - frag - il - is - tic - ex - pi - al - i - do - cious!

mp E - ven though the sound of it is some-thing quite a - tro - cious,

mf If you say it loud e - nough, you'll al - ways sound pre - co - cious.

f Sup - er - cal - i - frag - il - is - tic - ex - pi - al - i - do - cious!

p Um did - dle did - dle did - dle, um did - dle ay!

Um did - dle did - dle did - dle, um did - dle ay!

1. Be - cause I was a - fraid to speak when I was just a lad,

Me fa - ther gave me nose a tweak and told me I was bad.

But then one day I learned a word that saved me ach - in' nose,

D.C. al Fine

The big - gest word you ev - er 'eard and this is 'ow it goes: Oh!

2. 'E traveled all around the world and ev'rywhere 'e went
'E'd use his word and all would say, "There goes a clever gent!"
When dukes and maharajas pass the time of day with me,
I say me special word and then they ask me out to tea. Oh! *Refrain*

3. So when the cat has got your tongue, there's no need for dismay.
Just summon up this word and then you've got a lot to say.
But better use it carefully or it can change your life.
One night I said it to me girl and now me girl's me wife. Oh! *Refrain*

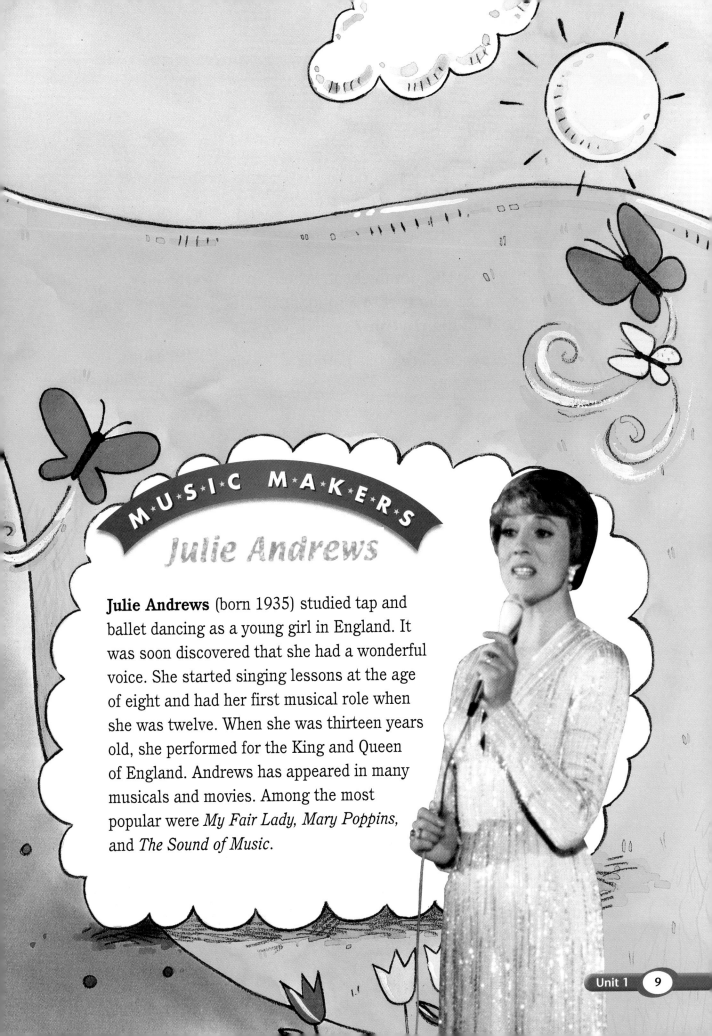

M·U·S·I·C M·A·K·E·R·S

Julie Andrews

Julie Andrews (born 1935) studied tap and ballet dancing as a young girl in England. It was soon discovered that she had a wonderful voice. She started singing lessons at the age of eight and had her first musical role when she was twelve. When she was thirteen years old, she performed for the King and Queen of England. Andrews has appeared in many musicals and movies. Among the most popular were *My Fair Lady*, *Mary Poppins*, and *The Sound of Music*.

What's in a Name? RHYTHM!

You've got rhythm. You've also got the beat. When you clap your hands or tap your foot to a song, are you clapping the **beat** or the **rhythm?**

Say the words of this speech piece while patting your knees to the steady beat.

> The **beat** is the regular pulse felt in most music.

> **Rhythm** is a pattern of long and short sounds and silences.

1-6

Name, Name, What's Your Name?

By Jim Solomon

Name, name, what's your name? Say it now, we'll play a game.

Say it high, say it low, an-y old way, but don't be slow.

Names to Play

Different names can have different rhythms.
Look at the examples below.

$\frac{2}{4}$ Pra - nav, Pra - nav

$\frac{2}{4}$ Joe, Joe

$\frac{2}{4}$ Mar - i - sol, Mar - i - sol

What rhythm do you hear in your name?

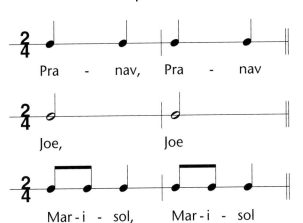

William Shakespeare wrote, "What's in a name? That which we call a rose by any other name would smell as sweet." What do you think he meant?

Rhythms to Play

Play these rhythm patterns with "Name, Name, What's Your Name?" Choose a rhythm instrument for each pattern.

1. $\frac{2}{4}$

2. $\frac{2}{4}$

3. $\frac{2}{4}$

Frog Rhythms

Some rhythms have one sound on a beat.   ♩ quarter note

Some rhythms have two sounds on a beat.   ♫ eighth notes

Sometimes there are no sounds at all on a beat.   𝄽 quarter rest

This song has all three rhythms. Look for these rhythms as you **sing** "Frog in the Millpond."

 1-8

Frog in the Millpond

Additional Verses by Bryan Louiselle   *Traditional Song from the United States*

1. Frog in the mill - pond, Can't get him out.

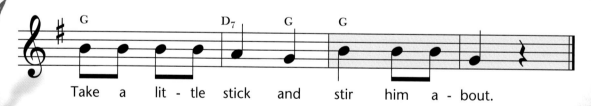

Take a lit - tle stick and stir him a - bout.

2. Frog in the millpond,
    Hops pretty quick.
    Better use a net;
    He doesn't like the stick.

3. Frog in the millpond,
    Hides in the muck.
    Broke out of the net
    with froggie kind of luck.

Feel the Rhythm

Look at the song again. **Sing** the part that is in green and tap a steady beat on each lily pad below. Clap the words to feel the rhythm.

stir   him a -   bout

Stir Up the Rhythm

The rhythms to the first line of the song are stirred up here. Can you find the line that matches the song?

Create a Frog Rhythm

Create your own frog rhythm using

♩, ♫, and 𝄽.

Move to show the rhythm you created.

Perform your frog rhythm for your class on rhythm sticks.

Four Sounds on a Beat

Rhythms come in many combinations.
Here's a song with a new one!

1-10 Ding, Dong, Diggidiggidong

English Version Adapted by Margaret Murray

From Orff-Keetman, Orff-Schulwerk, Vol. 1

Ding, dong, dig-gi-dig-gi-dong, Dig-gi-dig-gi-dong, the cat she's gone.

Ding, dong, dig-gi-dig-gi-dong, Dig-gi-dig-gi-ding dang dong.

Which word has four sounds on a beat?

Ding,   **dong,**   **dig-gi-dig-gi-**   **dong,**

The rhythm that has four sounds on a beat looks like this: ♩♪♪♪♪

Sing the song and point to the notes as you sing. Find each ♩♪♪♪♪ in the song.

Sing the song again with rhythm syllables as you clap the rhythm.

Tune In

Folklore tells us cats have nine lives. Actually, their spines are very flexible, so they can twist to land on their feet and escape danger.

14

Hear the Bells

Listen to another version of "Ding, Dong, Diggidiggidong." How is it different from the way you sang it?

1-12
Ding, Dong, Diggidiggidong

from Orff-Keetman, *Orff-Schulwerk, Vol. 1*

This version is accompanied by xylophone, cello, and timpani.

Cats

(excerpt)
by Eleanor Farjeon

Cats sleep
Anywhere,
Any table,
Any chair,
Top of piano,
Window-ledge,
In the middle,
On the edge.

Show What You Know!

Sing this pattern with rhythm syllables first. Then **sing** the pitch syllables. Now **sing** the words while you **play** the pattern on a xylophone.

mi mi mi mi re mi do
dig-gi-dig-gi-ding dang dong.

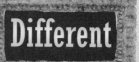

Same   Same   Different   Same

This French song has four lines of music. Each line is a **phrase. Sing** to discover which of the phrases in *"Au clair de la lune"* sound alike. Do they look alike, too?

A **phrase** is a musical sentence.

1-13

Au clair de la lune
(In the Moonlight)

English Version by D. Auberge   *Traditional Song from France*

Au clair de la lu - ne, Mon a - mi Pier - rot,
Stand-ing in the moon - light, Mon a - mi Pier - rot,

Prê - te - moi ta plu - me, Pour é - crire un mot;
I have lost my can - dle, How, I do not know!

Ma chan - delle est mor - te je n'ai plus de feu.
If you can - not help me, I will have to stay

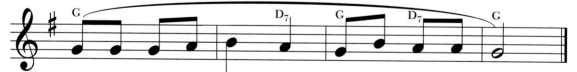

Ou - vre - moi ta por - te, Pour l'a - mour de Dieu.
Stand-ing in the dark - ness, 'til the light of day.

Follow the Phrases

Listen for the phrases that are alike as you follow the listening map.

1-17

Ah, vous dirai-je, Maman

**from *12 Variations in C, K. 265/300e*
by Wolfgang Amadeus Mozart**

Mozart [MOHT-zahrt] based this piano piece on a French folk song. You may know this song as "Twinkle, Twinkle, Little Star."

Ah, vous dirai-je, Maman
Listening Map

Unlock the Form

How many sections do you see in this song?
Listen to find the **form.**

Form is the overall plan of a piece of music.

1-18

Ambos a dos
(Go Two by Two)

English Words by Aura Kontra   *Folk Song from Latin America*

Am - bos   a   dos,   ma - ta - ri - le,   ri - le,   ri - le,
Go   two   by   two,   ma - ta - ri - le,   ri - le,   ri - le,

Am - bos   a   dos,   ma - ta - ri - le,   ri - le,   ron.
Go   two   by   two,   ma - ta - ri - le,   ri - le,   ron.

1.   Yo   ten-go un   cas - ti - llo, ma - ta - ri - le,   ri - le,   ri - le,
1.   Come in - to   my   cas - tle, ma - ta - ri - le,   ri - le,   ri - le,

Yo   ten-go un   cas - ti - llo, ma - ta - ri - le,   ri - le,   ron,   pon,   pon.
Come in - to   my   cas - tle, ma - ta - ri - le,   ri - le,   ron,   pon,   pon.

2.   ¿Dónde están las llaves? . . .   2.   Where's the key to the door? . . . .
      ¿Dónde están las llaves? . . .   Where's the key to the door? . . . .

Play with Form

Play this part on your recorder when you hear the **A** section.

Move to the Form

The pictures show one way to play a game with this song. **Move** to show the two different sections in the song.

Did I hear a violin on that recording?

Dancing in the Rain

The notes of a melody can go up, go down, or stay the same. In what direction do the notes in the red color box go? The green color box?

1-21

I Don't Care If the Rain Comes Down

Traditional Folk Song from the United States

I don't care if the rain comes down,   I'm gon-na dance all day.

I don't care if the rain comes down,   I'm gon-na dance all   day.

Hey,   hey,   car-ry me a-way.   I'm gon-na dance all   day.

Hey,   hey,   car-ry me a-way.   I'm gon-na dance all   day.

20

Move in the Rain

This dance is called a "partner mixer" because you change partners. Try the dance with "I Don't Care If the Rain Comes Down."

Play in the Rain

Play the parts of the song in the color boxes on a xylophone. What other parts of the song can you play using these notes?

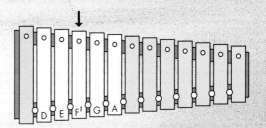

Music for the Rain

Listen to the *Raindrop Prelude.* What did the composer do to make this piece sound like rain?

1-25
Raindrop Prelude

by Frédéric Chopin

The *Raindrop Prelude* is one of twenty-four preludes written by Chopin [SHOH-pan]. A prelude, in Chopin's time, was simply a short musical piece.

Look at this small part of the *Raindrop Prelude.* Where is the part that sounds like rain?

Web Site Visit *www.sbgmusic.com* to find out more about Frédéric Chopin.

Did you know that there must be particles in the air, like dust, for rain to form?

MUSIC MAKERS

Frédéric Chopin

Frédéric Chopin (1810–1849) was born in Poland. As a child, he first showed his interest in the piano by asking questions during his older sister's lessons. When his parents realized he was quite talented, they let Chopin have his own piano lessons. Because Chopin was very shy, he enjoyed writing music more than performing. He loved the piano, and wrote almost all of his music— over 200 pieces—for the piano.

Notes to Know

The *Chorus* parts of this African American spiritual use only three notes: *mi, re,* and *do.* **Sing** the pitch syllables for all the parts of the song marked *Chorus.* **Sing** words for the parts marked *Solo.*

1-26

Oh, Won't You Sit Down

African American Spiritual

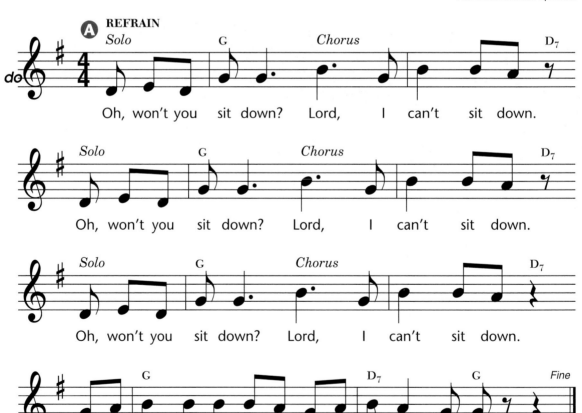

A REFRAIN

Solo ... G ... *Chorus* ... D₇

Oh, won't you sit down? Lord, I can't sit down.

Solo ... G ... *Chorus* ... D₇

Oh, won't you sit down? Lord, I can't sit down.

Solo ... G ... *Chorus* ... D₇

Oh, won't you sit down? Lord, I can't sit down.

G ... D₇ ... G ... *Fine*

'Cause I just got to Heav-en, gon-na look a-round. __

Reading *do re mi*

In this song, *do* is on the second line of the staff. Find *re* and *mi*.

do   ___   ___

Which is the lowest pitch?
Which is the highest?

B **VERSE**
Solo

1. Who's that yon - der dressed in red? ___

Chorus

Must be the chil - dren that ___ Mo - ses led. ___

Solo

Who's that yon - der dressed in white? ___

Chorus   *D.C. al Fine*

Must be the chil - dren of the Is - rael - ite. ___

2. Who's that yonder dressed in blue?
    Must be the children that are comin' through.
    Who's that yonder dressed in black?
    Must be the hypocrites a-turnin' back. *Refrain*

Come on Home

Sing "Ida Red" with pitch syllables and hand signs.

Find the five different pitches in the song. What is the last note of the song? Since this song has five different pitches and ends on *do,* we say the song is in *do* **pentatonic.**

Songs that have only five pitches are sometimes called **pentatonic.**

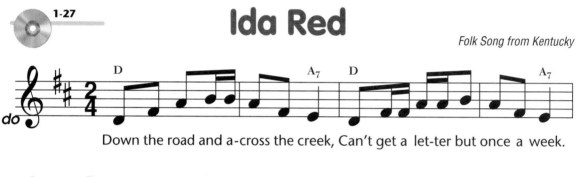

1-27

Ida Red

Folk Song from Kentucky

Down the road and a-cross the creek, Can't get a let-ter but once a week.

I - da Red, I - da Blue, I got stuck on I - da, too.

Show What You Know!

- Add pitch syllables to these phrases to **create** your own pentatonic song.

- Use the pitches *do, re, mi, so,* and *la.*

- To make the song sound complete, the last pitch must be *do.* End the other phrases on a different pitch.

Sing your compositions or **play** them on a mallet instrument.

How Many Voices?

This song has a verse and a refrain. **Listen** carefully to the voices that sing each part. When do you hear a solo? When do you hear a group?

Mud

1-29

Words by Marilyn Singer

Music by David Eddleman

REFRAIN

This stick here, that stick there.__ Mud, more mud, add mud, good mud.__

This stick here,   that stick there.__ Mud, more mud, add mud, good mud. __

VERSE

1. You pat.   I gnaw.   I pile.   You store.
2. You guard.   I pack.   I dig.   You stack.
3. I trim.   You mold   to keep   out cold.

D. C. al Fine

You pat.   I gnaw.   I pile.   You store.
You guard.   I pack.   I dig.   You stack.
I trim.   You mold   to keep   out cold.

Name That Voice

Listen to another song with a verse and refrain. Which part is sung by a man? Which part is sung by a group? **Sing** along when the group sings.

1-31
The Hippopotamus Song

by Michael Flanders and Donald Swann

The Hippopotamus Song is part of a show called *At the Drop of a Hat*. The show opened in 1956 and ran for over ten years.

The Hippopotamus Song

by Michael Flanders and Donald Swann

Verse
A bold hippopotamus was standing one day
On the banks of the cool Shalimar.
He gazed at the bottom as it peacefully lay
By the light of the evening star.
Away on a hilltop sat, combing her hair,
His fair hippopotamine maid.
The hippopotamus was no ignoramus
And sang her this sweet serenade.

Refrain
Mud, mud, glorious mud,
Nothing quite like it for cooling the blood.
So follow me, follow, down to the hollow
And there let us wallow in glorious mud.

Michael Flanders and Donald Swann

Michael Flanders (on the right) (1922–1975) and **Donald Swann** (1923–1994) first performed together during their college years in England. Swann was a pianist, and Flanders was an actor. After serving in World War II, they started performing together again. They wrote and sang their songs in musical revues for many years. Their music is always funny and clever.

A Poem to Read with a Friend

Choose a partner to read this poem with you. When the words on the left and the right line up, you read together. When they don't, you read alone. Read carefully!

Grasshoppers

by Paul Fleischman

Sap's rising	
	Ground's warming
Grasshoppers are	Grasshoppers are
hatching out	hatching out
Autumn-laid eggs	
	splitting
Young stepping	into spring
	Grasshoppers
Grasshoppers	hopping
hopping	
high	Grassjumpers
Grassjumpers	jumping
jumping	far
Vaulting from	
leaf to leaf	
stem to stem	leaf to leaf
plant to plant	stem to stem
	Grass
leapers	leapers
Grass	
bounders	bounders
	Grass-
springers	springers
Grass	
soarers	soarers
Leapfrogging	Leapfrogging
longjumping	longjumping
grasshoppers.	grasshoppers.

Alone or Together?

Sometimes you sing alone. Sometimes a musical instrument plays along with your singing.

Listen to two recordings of "Make New Friends." In one, the singers sing alone. In the other, you will hear an **accompaniment.** A string quartet, four string instruments, plays along. The lowest sounding instrument is the cello [CHEL-oh].

> An **accompaniment** is a part that supports a main melody. It is usually played by one or more instruments.

1-32

Make New Friends

Traditional Round

Make new friends, but keep ___ the ___ old, ___

One is sil - ver and the oth - er gold.

make

Sing and Sign Together

Now **sing** the song yourself. Practice signing it as you sing.

new

friends

Playing Alone

Listen to Yo-Yo Ma play a cello solo without accompaniment.

1-35

Bourée 1

from *Suite No. 3 in C Major for Unaccompanied Cello* by Johann Sebastian Bach

Bach [bahk] composed a series of pieces for solo cello.

M·U·S·I·C M·A·K·E·R·S

Yo-Yo Ma

Yo-Yo Ma (born 1955) was born in Paris into a musical family. His father was a violinist. His mother was a singer. He began playing the cello when he was very young. When the Ma family moved to the United States, Yo-Yo's parents enrolled him at the famous Juilliard School of Music in New York City. He was only nine years old at the time.

Ma has played as a soloist with many great orchestras. He also plays recitals and performs with other famous musicians from the fields of jazz and popular music.

Playing with Friends

Now **listen** to Yo-Yo Ma play with an accompaniment. What instrument plays with him?

1-36
Mit Humor

**from *5 Stücke im Volkston*
by Robert Schumann**

Robert Schumann [SHOO-mahn] composed this piece to be accompanied by the piano.

Yo-Yo Ma can also perform as an accompanist. **Listen** to how he accompanies the singing of Bobby McFerrin.

1-37
Musette

by Johann Sebastian Bach

A musette is a dance. It is also a kind of bagpipe. Can you hear the drone of the bagpipe in the cello part?

Web Site Go to *www.sbgmusic.com* to find out more about Yo-Yo Ma and Bobby McFerrin.

Musical Marketplace

In Latin America, outdoor marketplaces, or flea markets, are very colorful. People sell many things there. **Sing** this song about a flea market where musical instruments are sold.

1-38

La pulga de San José

Adapted Spanish words by José-Luis Orozco

Musical arrangement by José-Luis Orozco
Folk Song from Latin America

En la pul - ga de San Jo - sé

yo com - pré u - na gui - ta - rra,

ta - ra, ta - ra, ta - rra, la gui - ta - rra.

Va - ya u - sted, va - ya u - sted

Play in the Market

Play these **ostinatos** as you **sing** this song. Add one part at a time. Choose an instrument you would like to hear with the song.

> An **ostinato** is a repeated rhythm or melody pattern.

1.

2.

a la pul - ga de San Jo - sé.

Va - ya u - sted, va - ya u - sted

a la pul - ga de San Jo - sé.

2. *En la pulga de San José,*
   yo compré un clarinete,
   nete, nete, nete, el clarinete,
   tara, tara, tarra, la guitarra. Refrain

3. *En la pulga de San José,*
   yo compré un violín,
   lin, lin, lin, el violín,
   nete, nete, nete, el clarinete,
   tara, tara, tarra, la guitarra. Refrain

Putting It

What Do You Know?

1. Look at the notation of *"Au clair de la lune"* on page 16.

   a. Point to two pitches that show the melody moving up.

   b. Point to two pitches that show the melody moving down.

   c. Point to two pitches that show the melody repeating.

2. Which of these patterns shows AB form?

   a. ● ■ ●   **c.** ● ■

   b. ● ●   **d.** ● ■ ▲

1-40

What Do You Hear? 1

You will hear five musical examples. Does the end of each phrase move up, move down, or stay the same?

1.	up	down	same
2.	up	down	same
3.	up	down	same
4.	up	down	same
5.	up	down	same

All Together

What You Can Do

Sing and Move with Expression

Sing "I Don't Care If the Rain Comes Down" on page 20.

- Sing the first two lines *piano.* Use small steady beat movements as you sing.

- Sing the last two lines *forte.* Use large steady beat movements as you sing.

Perform Rhythmic Ostinatos

Sing "Ding, Dong, Diggidiggidong" on page 14 with the recording. Softly pat one of these three ostinatos as you sing.

a.

b.

c.

Create a Melody

- Create a melody for the poem, "Rain," using ♩ , ♫ , and 𝄽 .

- Use these pitches.

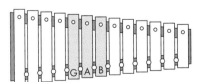

by Robert Louis Stevenson
The rain is raining all around,
It falls on field and tree,
It rains on the umbrellas here,
And on the ships at sea.

- Teach your friends to sing your melody.

Listening for *Style*

Reggae [REH-gay] is a **style** of music that combines the sound of American pop music with African-based Jamaican sounds. Reggae accompaniments often include short ostinatos played on keyboard, electric guitar, bass, and drums. Bob Marley was an important reggae composer and performer.

Bob Marley

Robert Nesta (Bob) Marley (1945–1981) was born in Jamaica. He grew up playing music, and at 16 years of age he made his first recording. Soon after, Marley, his best friend Bunny Livingston, and several other musicians formed a band called the Wailers. Bob Marley and the Wailers made reggae music known all over the world.

Marley's music is known for being about social issues such as unity and peace. In 1978 Marley was awarded the Peace Medal of the Third World from the United Nations.

Exploring MuSic

Sing Like a Bird

Listen for the spaces, or rests, in the song. What do the rests do for the song? What makes this song sound like reggae style?

2-1

Three Little Birds

Words and Music by Bob Marley

REFRAIN

Don't wor - ry　　　　a - bout　a thing

'cause ev-'ry lit-tle thing　　gon-na be all right.

Sing-in' don't wor - ry　　　　a-bout　a thing

'cause ev-'ry lit-tle thing　　gon-na be all right.

42

VERSE

Rise up this morn-ing,   smile __ with the ris - ing sun.

Three __ lit - tle birds   sit by my door-step,

Sing-in' sweet __ songs   of mel-o-dies pure and true,

D. S. al Fine

Sing-in':   "This is my mes-sage to you-hoo-hoo."   Sing-in' don't

TRAIN TO FREEDOM

Many African American spirituals were used to send messages along the Underground Railroad. What message does this song send? **Listen** to "Train Is A-Comin'." **Sing** the song and learn all the verses.

2-3

Train Is A-Comin'

African American Spiritual

1. Train   is   a - com - in',   oh,   yes,
2. Better   get   your   tick - et,   oh,   yes,

Train   is   a - com - in', _____   oh,   yes,
Better   get   your   tick - et, _____   oh,   yes,

Get on Board!

Play these ostinatos with the song.

On the first verse, use the cabasa. On the second verse, add the vibraslap. On the third verse, you can add the drum.

Train   is   a - com - in',   train   is   a - com - in',
Better   get   your   tick - et,   better   get   your   tick - et,

Train   is   a - com - in',   oh,   yes.
Better   get   your   tick - et,   oh,   yes.

3. Room for many others, oh, yes,
   Room for many others, oh, yes,
   Room for many others, room for many others,
   Room for many others, oh, yes.

Fast or Slow—Go, Beat, Go!

Have you ever thought about how different songs go at different speeds? In music, we call this the **tempo** of a song.

Here are some words musicians use for tempo.

adagio	= slow
moderato	= medium
allegro	= fast
accelerando	= getting faster
ritardando	= getting slower

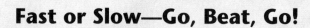

MUSIC MAKERS

Joseph Joubert

Joseph Joubert [zhoo-BARE] (born 1958) is a pianist, composer, arranger, and accompanist. He began piano lessons at age eight. At the young age of sixteen, he performed in New York City with full orchestra. He accompanied singer Kathleen Battle in recital at the White House for the American and Russian presidents in 1994. His musical arrangements in this book include "Hush, Hush," "Children, Go Where I Send Thee," and "Little Johnny Brown." Joubert lives in New Jersey.

2-5

Interview with Joseph Joubert

Same Song, But Different

Choo-Choo Joubert is based on "Train Is A-Comin'."
Listen for the different tempos in the song as you
follow the listening map.

2-6

Choo-Choo Joubert

by Joseph Joubert

The form of this piece is theme and variation. How many different
ways does the composer use the melody?

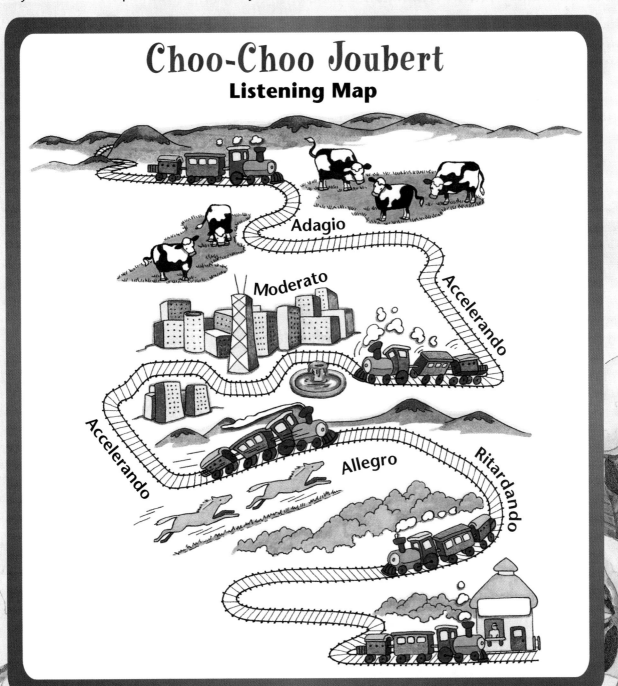

SNEAKY SNAKE RHYTHM

Some snakes like to hide in tall grass. These snakes like to hide in rhythms. Find the snakes hiding in the rhythm patterns below. Each snake ties two notes together.

Tune In

Snakes have no eyelids, so they can't blink. They also can't hear, so a rattlesnake doesn't hear its own rattle!

Tie It Together!

The song below is written with **ties** instead of snakes. **Read** the rhythm of "Black Snake."

A **tie** is a musical symbol that joins two notes together to create a longer sound.

 2-7

Black Snake

Traditional

Black snake, black snake, where are ___ you hid - ing?

Black snake, black snake, where are ___ you hid - ing?

Black snake, black snake, where are ___ you hid - ing?

Don't you bite _____ me! _____

Two Beats, Three Sounds

The highlighted measure has the new rhythm pattern with three sounds. Which sound is the longest?

Name the New Rhythm

"Mister Ram Goat-O" is a song from Trinidad. In Caribbean songs, animals are sometimes called Mister, brother, or some other title of respect.

Listen to the recording of "Mister Ram Goat-O" and **sing** and clap on the word *Bam-ban-dy-a.*

Mister Ram Goat-O

2-8

Folk Song from Trinidad

Mis - ter Ram Goat - O! Bam - ban - dy - a. Mis - ter

Ram Goat - O! Bam - ban - dy - a. Can you

lend me a ra - zor? Bam - ban - dy - a. It's to

shave off my long beard. Bam - ban - dy - a.

Musical Homonyms

There are different ways to write rhythms that sound the same.

This pattern can also be written like this:

The new rhythm can also be written like this:

What rhythm do you know that sounds the same as ♪ ♪?

The new rhythm pattern can also be written like this: ♪ ♩ ♪

This rhythm pattern is called **syncopation**.

Syncopation is a rhythm in which the note that is stressed comes between two beats.

Find the syncopation in "Mister Ram Goat-O." Then sing the song and clap the syncopated patterns.

Now Hear the Rhythm

This song is about *Carnaval,* a festival celebrated in many Spanish-speaking countries. Look at the notation. How many syncopated rhythms do you find? **Sing** the song.

2-10

Ahora voy a cantarles

English Words by Alice Firgau

(Now Hear the Song)

Folk Song from Argentina

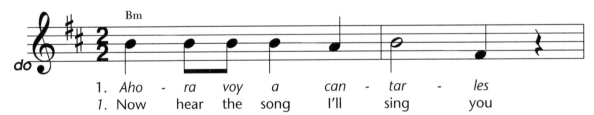

1. *Aho - ra voy a can - tar - les*
1. Now hear the song I'll sing you

has - ta que a - pun - te el lu - ce - ro.
Un - til the dawn is ____ break - ing.

Show What You Know!

Clap and say these patterns with rhythm syllables. Then **play** them on percussion instruments with *"Ahora voy a cantarles."*

1. (rhythm pattern in 4/4)

2. (rhythm pattern in 4/4)

Los car - na - va - les ya vie - nen
All through the night hap - py peo - ple

des - de la ci - ma del ce - rro.
Come down from on the ___ moun - tain.

2. ¡Todos, toditos, arriba!
   ¡El carnaval ha llegado!
   Domingo, lunes y martes,
   tres días y se acabó.

2. Come on, my friends, come join me.
   Carnaval time is here now,
   Sunday and Monday and Tuesday,
   Three days, no more 'til next year.

FOLLOW THE LEADER

"Great Day" is a **call-and-response** song. **Listen** to the song and clap the responses.

Then clap the calls and **sing** the responses. Use dynamics!

Call and response is a form of choral singing. The call is sung by a leader and the response is usually sung by a group.

GREAT DAY

2-14

African American Spiritual

REFRAIN
Great __ day! Great day, the right-eous march-in'.

Great __ day! God's gon-na build up Zi - on's walls.

VERSE
Call
1. The char - iot rode on the moun - tain top, __
2. This is the day of __ ju - bi - lee, __

Call to Move!

Move to this pattern on the response phrases in "Great Day."

God's gonna   build up   Zion's   walls

Response

God's gon - na build up   Zi - on's walls.

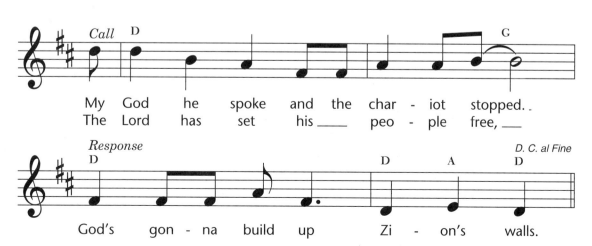

Call

My God he spoke and the char - iot stopped.
The Lord has set his ___ peo - ple free, ___

Response   *D. C. al Fine*

God's gon - na build up   Zi - on's walls.

Question and Answer Games

"John Kanaka" is a work song. It has been sung by dockworkers in California to keep rhythm while they load cargo.

Listen to "John Kanaka." Can you hear a repeating phrase?

2-16

John Kanaka

Sea Shanty

I heard, I heard the old man say,

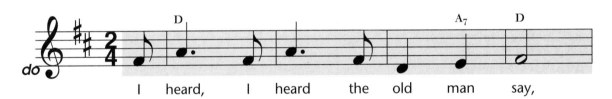

John Ka - na - ka, na - ka, too - lai - ay.

To - day, to - day is a hol - i - day,

See the Question?

You remember that a phrase is a musical sentence. In music, we often have a phrase that asks a musical question, then a phrase that gives an answer.

Sing the first phrase of "John Kanaka," using pitch syllables. On what pitch does the phrase end? Does it sound finished? This is the question phrase.

Find the Answer?

Now sing the second phrase of the song, using pitch syllables. On what pitch does this phrase end? An answer phrase often ends on *do*.

Identify all the question and answer phrases in "John Kanaka." Some of your class can sing the question phrases, while others sing the answer phrases. A small group can play the question and answer rhythms on their recorders, using the pitch "A".

Play with Me

Play an accompaniment to "John Kanaka." Some of your classmates can sing the song, while the others play.

Dance with Me

Now try these dance steps to "John Kanaka."

Lines 1 and 3: Do a slide-close. ▶

◀ Lines 2, 4, and 6: Do a clapping pattern.

Line 5: Do a right-arm swing. ▶

Listen to the Dance

Bransle de la Torche has twelve question phrases and twelve answer phrases.

2-18
Bransle de la Torche

**from *Dances from Terpsichore*
by Michael Praetorius**

Michael Praetorius wrote this piece in 1612.

Step This Way

When you move, sometimes you take big steps. Sometimes you take little steps. You can skip or step in place. A melody also moves. It can move in small steps, skips, or stay in one place.

Sing this famous dance song from the pop music of the 1960s. You may already know it!

2-19

The Loco-Motion

Words and Music by Gerry Goffin and Carole King

A — Eb — Cm

Ev - 'ry - bo - dy's do - in' a brand - new dance __ now,
Move a - round the floor __ in a lo - co - mo - tion,

Eb — Cm

Come on, ba - by, do ___ the lo - co - mo - tion. I

Eb — Cm

know you'll get to like it if you give it a chance __ now,
Do it hold - in' hands __ if ___ you get the no - tion,

Eb — Cm

Come on, ba - by, do ___ the lo - co - mo - tion.

Melody Moves

Can you find these steps, skips, and repeated pitches in "The Loco-Motion"?

step

skip

repeat

You've got the knack!

My lit-tle ba-by sis-ter can do it with ease, _ It's
There's nev-er been a dance _ that's so eas-y to do, _ It

eas-i-er than learn-in' your A B C's. _ So
e-ven makes you hap-py when you're feel-in' blue. _

come on, come on, do _ the lo-co-mo-tion with me. _

You got-ta swing your hips now, _ Come on, ba-by, Jump up,

jump back, Oh, well, I think you got the knack. _

Do the Loco-Motion!

Now it's time to learn the dance steps to "The Loco-Motion."
As you **move**, make a chugging motion with your arms.

Everybody's doing a brand-new dance now,

Come on, baby, do the locomotion.

Beautiful Music

Listen to another song written by Carole King.

2-21
Beautiful

by Carole King

Beautiful is one of the most famous songs from Carole King's album *Tapestry.*

MUSIC MAKERS

CAROLE KING

Carole King (born 1942) has had a career in music since the 1950s. Her first songs were ready to be published while she was just a teenager. With Gerry Goffin, she wrote many popular songs, including "The Loco-Motion." She has also written and recorded her music on her own. One of her albums, *Tapestry,* sold millions of copies.

Morning Melodies

"One Morning Soon" is an African American spiritual, a religious folk song. All the pitch syllables you know are in this song, plus a new note!

Sing the first three measures of the song with pitch syllables and hand signs. Here's a hint: The song starts on *do*.

 2-22

One Morning Soon

African American Spiritual

1. One morn - in' soon, ___ one morn - in' soon, ___
2. Down on my knees, ___ down on my knees, ___
3. One day 'bout noon, ___ one day 'bout noon, ___

One morn - in' soon,
Down on my knees,   I   heard the   an - gels sing - in'.
One day 'bout noon,

Skip Down to a New Note

Now **sing** the last measure of the song with words and **listen** for a new note. Does the note sound higher or lower than *do?* Find the new note in the song.

Since the new note is a skip below *do,* where will the new note go on each of the staffs below?

do   ?   do

do   ?   do

do   ?   do

On This Day
by M. B. Goffstein

On this day
I'm going to pick
a big bouquet
and put it in my shoe
and let it sail away.
And when it gets
across the sea,
how amazed the children
there
will be.

Name the New Note

The new note that is a skip below *do* is low *la.*

Play this pattern on a bass xylophone.

Then **create** an ostinato to play as a **B** section for "One Morning Soon." Use the pitches above.

Find the New Note

"*Hosisipa*" is a Sioux hand game song. **Listen** to the recording, and then **sing** the song.

2-24

Hosisipa

Native American Game Song of the Sioux

Ho - si - si - pa, ho - si - si - pa, ho - si - si - pa, ho - si.

Arts Connection

This doll and cradle board were made by the Dakota Sioux in the 1800s.

Sign the New Note

In *"Hosisipa,"* do is on the second line. On what note does the song end? **Sing** *"Hosisipa"* with pitch syllables and hand signs.

mi   re   do   la

Show What You Know!

Sing each example with pitch syllables and hand signs. Then **play** them on resonator bells.

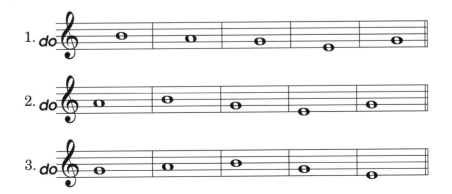

1. do
2. do
3. do

Exploring

Everyone has a family tree. Mother, brothers, aunts, and cousins are all part of your family tree. **Sing** "Family Tree." What family members does the singer include in his story?

Family Tree

2-25

Words and Music by John Forster and Tom Chapin

VERSE

1. Be-fore the days of Jell-O lived a pre-his-tor-ic fel-low
2. My grand-pa came from Rus-sia; my grand-ma came from Prus-sia;
3. One fine day I may go to Tie-rra del Fue-go.

Who loved a maid and court-ed her be-neath the ban-yan tree.
They met in No-va Sco-tia, had my dad in Ten-nes-see.
Per-haps I'll meet my wife there and we'll move to Tim-buk-tu.

And they had lots of chil-dren and their chil-dren all had chil-dren.
Then they moved to Yo-ko-ha-ma, where Dad-dy met my ma-ma.
And our kid will be bi-ling-ual, and though she may stay sin-gle,

And they kept on hav-ing chil-dren un-til one of them had me.
Her dad's from Al-a-bam-a and her mom's part Cher-o-kee.
She could, of course, go min-gle with the king of Kat-man-du.

Voices

REFRAIN

We're a fam - 'ly and we're a tree. Our
roots go deep down in ___ his - to - ry, from my
great - great - grand - dad - dy reach - in' up to me; ___ we're a
green and grow - ing ___ fam - 'ly tree.

Listen for a Special Sound

Each time you hear a new voice in this
song, you hear a different vocal **timbre.**
How many different timbres do you hear?

Timbre is the special
sound each voice or
instrument makes.

A Family 'Round the World

Some of the places listed here are named in "Family Tree." Speak each one.

Create a word chain using these place names. Combine two or more and speak them in rhythm. Try this!

Yokohama   Alabama
Madagascar   Tierra del Fuego
Russia   Alaska
Nova Scotia   Timbuktu
Tennessee

Yo - ko - ha - ma, Ma - da - gas - car, A - la - ba - ma, Tim - buk - tu.

Find Your Place in the World

The stars on the map show some of the places named above. Can you match a name to each star?

Web Site Go to *www.sbgmusic.com* to learn more about Tom Chapin and his music.

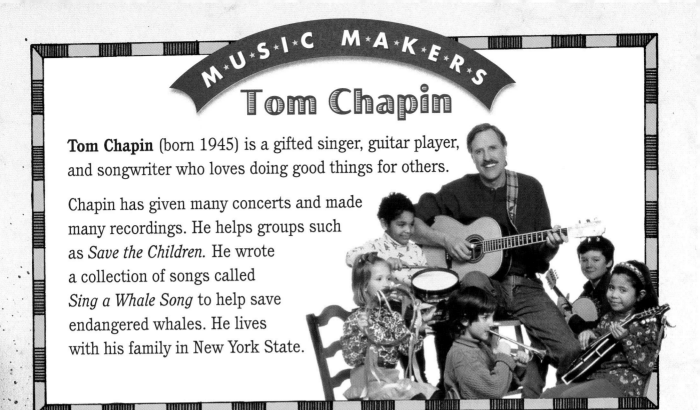

MUSIC MAKERS

Tom Chapin

Tom Chapin (born 1945) is a gifted singer, guitar player, and songwriter who loves doing good things for others.

Chapin has given many concerts and made many recordings. He helps groups such as *Save the Children.* He wrote a collection of songs called *Sing a Whale Song* to help save endangered whales. He lives with his family in New York State.

Element: TEXTURE/HARMONY | **Skill: SINGING** | **Connection: CULTURE**

Singing an

Have you ever called into a large, empty space and heard your voice echo back? Here's an echo song you can **sing** with your classmates.

I'm on My Way

African American Spiritual

1. I'm on my way (I'm on my way) to the free-dom land, (to the free-dom

land,) I'm on my way (I'm on my way) to the free-dom land, (to the free-dom

land,) I'm on my way (I'm on my way) to the free-dom land, (to the free-dom

land,) I'm on my way, __ thank God, I'm on my way. _____

2. I asked my friends . . . to go with me, . . . *(3 times)*
   I'm on my way, thank God, I'm on my way.

3. If they won't come . . . then I'll go alone, . . . *(3 times)*
   I'm on my way, thank God, I'm on my way.

4. I'm on my way . . . and I won't turn back, . . . *(3 times)*
   I'm on my way, thank God, I'm on my way.

ECHO ECHO ECHO ECHO

Moving in Echo

- **Move** your right arm in the shape of an arc when you sing the long notes on *way*.

- **Move** your left arm in an arc when you sing *land*.

- Make up your own move on the last line of the song.

Can you create different movements for the long notes?

Blankets of Sound

Sing this Slovakian lullaby. What words in this song suggest going to sleep?

2-29

Hej pada pada
(Dewdrops)

English Words by Ellen K. Traeger

Lullaby from Slovakia

Hej   pa - da   pa - da   ro - sic - ka,
Dew - drops a - fall - ing   from   the   skies,

Spa - ly   by   mo - je   o - cic - ka.
Drow - sy   and sleep - y,   close your eyes.

Spa - ly   by   mo - je,   Spa - ly   by   aj   tvo - je,
Drow - sy   and sleep - y, go   to   sleep my ba - by.

Spa - ly   by   du - sa   mo - ja   o - bo - je.
Dream of   the   dew - drops fall - ing from the skies.

Layer the Sound

Sing *"Hej pada pada"* without accompaniment. Now **sing** it again with the accompaniment. Every time you add another voice, or another instrument, you create a thicker **texture.**

Texture is how thin or thick music sounds. It is created by layering sounds on top of one another.

Playing with Texture

Play an accompaniment for the song on instruments. What instruments would you add to create a thicker texture?

Soprano Metallophone

Alto Metallophone

Bass Metallophone

More Slovakian Music

Listen to this piece by Leoš Janáček.

2-33
Moravian Dance No. 2

"Kalamajka" by Leoš Janáček

Moravia, like Slovakia, is part of the Czech Republic. Dance is an important part of Moravian life.

What Do You Know?

1. Match the musical terms with the correct definitions.

a. *adagio* • speed of the beat

b. *allegro* • slow

c. tempo • moderate (medium)

d. *moderato* • fast

2. Look at these patterns. Decide if each one is moving by step, skip, or repeated tone.

a.   **c.**   **e.**

b.   **d.**

2-34

What Do You Hear? 2

Listen to four musical examples.
Point to the word that best
describes the tempo of each example.

1. *accelerando*   *ritardando*

2. *allegro*   *adagio*

3. *allegro*   *adagio*

4. *accelerando*   *ritardando*

All Together

What You Can Do

Sing an Echo

Sing "I'm on My Way" with half the class singing the first part and the other half singing the echo. Be sure to hold, or sustain, the long notes.

Perform Call and Response

Perform this call-and-response speech piece with your classmates.

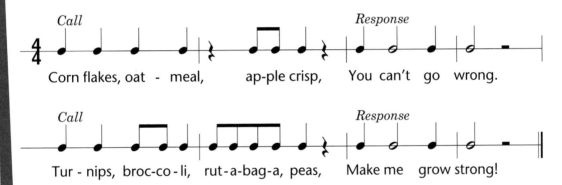

Call

Corn flakes, oat - meal,   ap-ple crisp,   You can't   go   wrong.

Response

Call

Tur - nips, broc-co-li,   rut-a-bag-a, peas,   Make me   grow strong!

Response

Create a Melody

Turn the speech piece into a song! Create a melody for your call-and-response piece. Use these pitches.

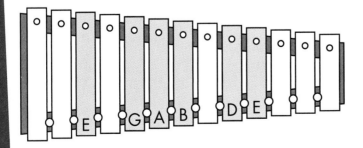

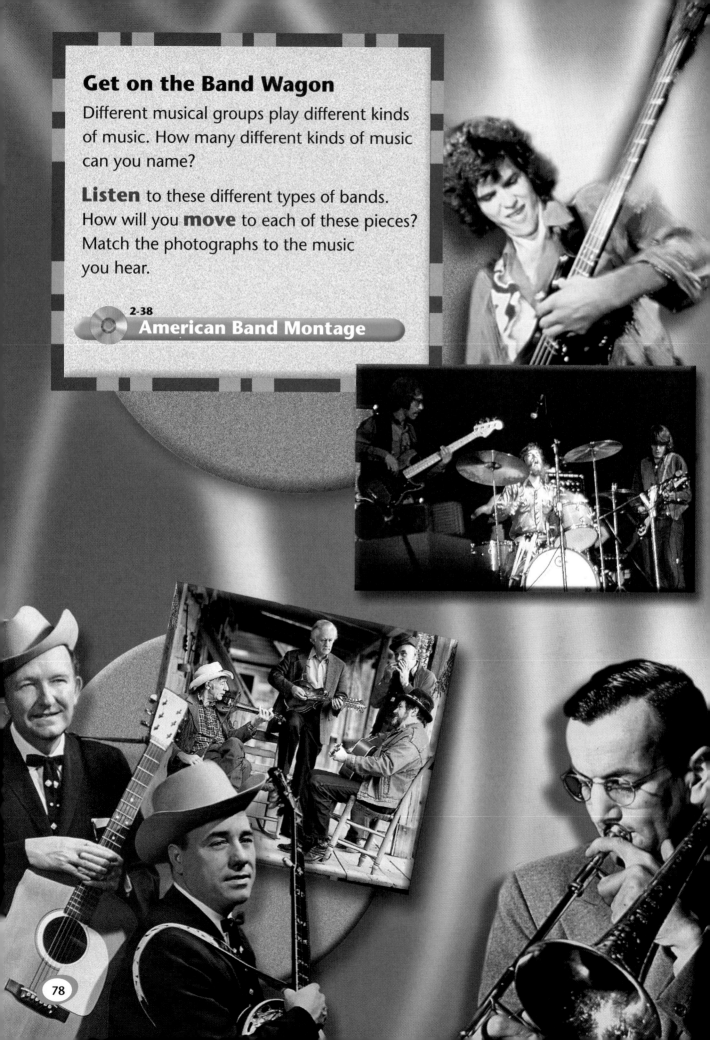

Get on the Band Wagon

Different musical groups play different kinds of music. How many different kinds of music can you name?

Listen to these different types of bands. How will you **move** to each of these pieces? Match the photographs to the music you hear.

2-38
American Band Montage

Learning the Language of MUSIC

Move to the Music

"Let's Get the Rhythm of the Band"
is made for dancing! **Move** the way the
words suggest as you **sing** the song.

2-39

Let's Get the Rhythm of the Band

Based on a Children's Rhyme

New Words and Music by Cheryl Warren Mattox

Let's get the rhy - thm of the band, oh yeah, _

We got the rhy - thm of the band. _____

Let's get the rhy - thm of the hand, clap your hands now,
snap your fin - gers,
wave your hands high,

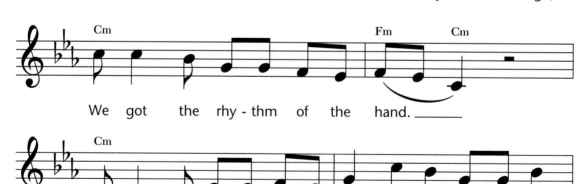

We got the rhy - thm of the hand. _____

Let's get the rhy - thm of the feet, stomp it out with me,
jump up high __ now,
march in time __ now,

We got the rhy-thm of the feet, _____

Let's get the rhy-thm of the band.

Let's get the rhy-thm of the band.

HOpS and Glides

Listen to "El gallo pinto" as it is sung in Spanish. What do you notice about the beginnings of the words in the last line? Have fun with the Spanish words as you learn to **sing** this song.

 3-1

El gallo pinto
(The Painted Rooster)

English Words by Jorge Winston-La Paz   *Spanish Words and Music by Tita Maya*

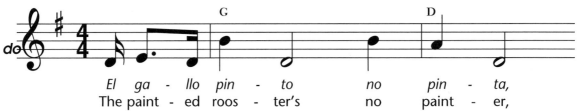

El   ga - llo   pin - to   no   pin - ta,
The paint - ed roos - ter's   no   paint - er,

El   que pin - ta   es   el   pin - tor;
For   the paint - er's   the one   who   paints;

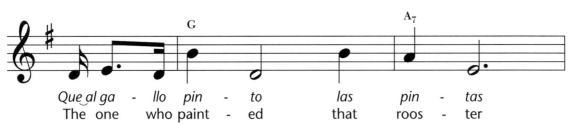

Que al ga - llo   pin - to   las   pin - tas
The one   who paint - ed   that   roos - ter

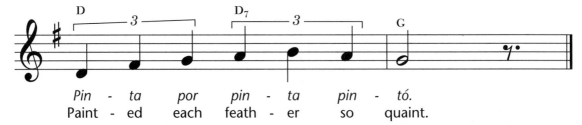

Pin - ta   por   pin - ta   pin - tó.
Paint - ed each feath - er   so   quaint.

Smooth or Separated?

Listen again to the recording of *"El gallo pinto."* You will hear the strings play ***legato*** and the trumpets play ***staccato***.

> **Legato** means "smooth and connected."

> **Staccato** means "short and separated."

Move to the Music

How would you **move** to this song? **Create** a dance for *legato* and *staccato* movements. You might use the movements shown below.

 MIDI Experiment with *legato* and *staccato* sounds in the accompaniment of *"El gallo pinto."*

The Long and Short of It

You can hear *staccato* and *legato* sounds in this piece.
Listen to the music and follow the listening map.
It shows the first two phrases of each section.

3-5

Gavotte

by François-Joseph Gossec

Gossec originally wrote this piece as a violin lesson for his
students. It is performed here by flute and orchestra.

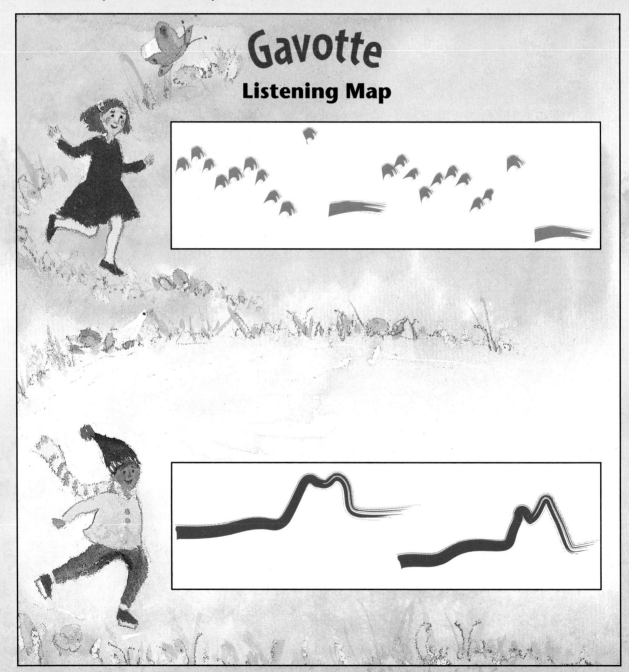

Gavotte
Listening Map

Styles in Art

Legato and *staccato* are words used to describe musical sounds that are smooth or separated. In art, you can *see* smooth and separated. These two paintings are examples of two different styles. The first one shows what is called a fluid, or smooth, line. The second uses a technique called pointillism, where the painter actually makes the entire picture out of dots of color.

Arts Connection

The Whirl
by Frantisek Kupka
(1871–1957) ▶

Arts Connection

Sous les Pins a Carqueiranne
by Louis Gaidan (1847–1925) ▼

▼ Close-up

Market Rhythms

Kingston is the capital city of Jamaica. "Kingston Market" tells about an outdoor market where many people shop.

Listen to the song to find the syncopated rhythm patterns.

Kingston Market

Words and Music by Irving Burgie

3-6

Have you ev - er seen a rain - bow or a

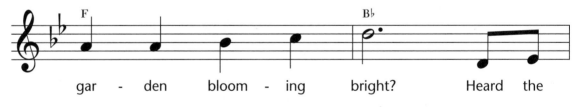

gar - den bloom - ing bright? Heard the

shuf - fle of a thou - sand feet or

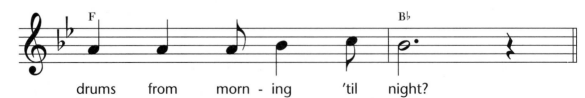

drums from morn - ing 'til night?

Jamaican Rhythm

In Jamaica, many groups of drummers play on the streets. **Play** this accompaniment on drums as you **sing** the song.

VERSE

REFRAIN

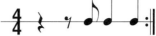

REFRAIN

B♭   E♭

Come we   go down,   come we   go down,

F   B♭

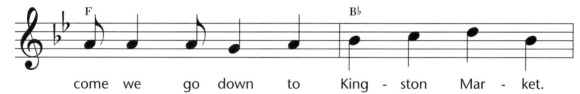

come we   go down   to   King - ston   Mar - ket.

B♭   E♭

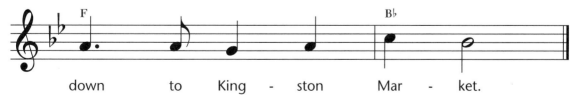

Come we   go down,   come we   go down,

F   B♭

down   to   King - ston   Mar - ket.

Chicken 'n' Rhythm

"Chicken on the Fence Post" is a song with silly words.
Sing the song and **move** to the music.

3-8

Chicken on the Fence Post

Play-Party Song from the United States

F

1. Chick - en   on   the   fence   post,   can't   dance   Jo - sey,

B♭   C

Chick - en   on   the   fence   post,   can't   dance   Jo - sey,

Clap Like a Chicken

Use rhythm syllables to say and clap the rhythm of the song. Which lines of rhythm are the same?

Chickens Composing!

Compose your own rhythm piece using ♩, ♫, and ♬. Use the same rhythm pattern for three lines of the piece, and a different rhythm for the fourth line. **Perform** your composition while the class sings the song.

Chick - en on the fence post, can't dance Jo - sey,

Hel - lo, Su - san Brown - y - o.

2. Choose my partner and come dance Josey, . . .

3. Chew my gum while I dance Josey, . . .

4. Shoestring's broke and I can't dance Josey, . . .

5. Hold my mule while I dance Josey, . . .

6. Hair in the butter, can't dance Josey, . . .

7. Briar in my heels, can't dance Josey, . . .

8. Stumped my toe, can't dance Josey, . . .

Love Those Rhythms!

Listen to "Love Somebody" and raise your hand when you hear ♩♩♩♩. Find the ♩♩♩♩ in the notation below. Then **sing** and clap the rhythm.

3-10

Love Somebody

Folk Song from the United States

Love some-bod - y, yes, I do, Love some-bod - y, yes, I do,

Love some-bod - y, yes, I do, Love some-bod-y but I won't tell who!

More Rhythms to Love

Read and clap these rhythms. How many lines of rhythm are the same?

Clap the rhythms again as you sing "Love Somebody." Do the rhythms and the song end at the same time?

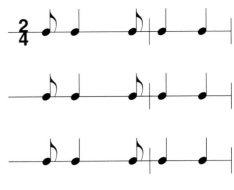

Did you know that Valentine's Day has been celebrated for 1,500 years?

Show What You Know!

Create your own four-beat rhythmic ostinato, using any of the rhythms below. **Play** your ostinato on percussion instruments as you **sing** "Love Somebody."

Which of the following rhythms last for one beat? Which rhythms last for two beats?

Songs of the Old West

"Old Dan Tucker" is an American frontier song.

Sing "Old Dan Tucker." **Listen** for two different sections of the song. What makes them different?

Old Dan Tucker

3-12

Folk Song from the United States

1. Old Dan Tuck-er was a might-y man, He

washed his face in the fry - ing pan,

Combed his hair with a wag - on wheel,

Had a tooth - ache in his heel;

A Two-Part Party Song

Look for the letters Ⓐ and Ⓑ in the song. A song that has two different sections is called two-part, or Ⓐ Ⓑ, form. In this song, the two sections are marked **Verse** and **Refrain**.

The **verse** of a song is a section where the melody stays the same even when the lyrics change.

The **refrain** of a song is sung the same way every time it repeats.

REFRAIN

So get out the way, Old Dan Tuck - er;

Get out the way, Old Dan Tuck - er;

Get out the way, Old Dan Tuck - er,

You're too late to get your sup - per.

2. Old Dan Tucker came to town,
   Riding a billy goat, leading a hound;
   Hound dog barked, then billy goat jumped;
   Dan fell off and landed on a stump; *Refrain*

Time to Play

With a partner, create ways to show **Ⓐ Ⓑ** form.
Here are a few ideas.

- **Move** a different way for each section.

- **Sing** the song and make the **Ⓑ** section louder or softer.

- **Play** this accompaniment during the verse. Then **create** your own part for the refrain.

Music for Dancing

Flop-Eared Mule is a dance tune from the Old West. Dance tunes were also known as "fiddle tunes" because they were created and played by violin players, or fiddlers. **Listen** to discover the form of the piece.

3-14
Flop-Eared Mule

Traditional American as performed by Don Wiles, Jim Widner, and Vivian Williams

This fiddle tune is a traditional melody.

Long ago, settlers held dances so people could get to know one another. The fiddle was the main instrument played for dances.

Element: FORM   **Skill: SINGING**   **Connection: SCIENCE**

Crocodile Form

Listen to this funny song from the musical film *Peter Pan*.

3-15

Words by Jack Lawrence

Never Smile at a Crocodile

Music by Frank Churchill

do

Nev - er smile at a croc - o - dile, No, you

can't get friend - ly with a croc - o - dile, Don't be

tak - en in by his wel - come grin, He's im -

ag - in - ing how well you'd fit with - in his skin.

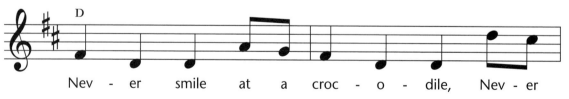

Nev - er smile at a croc - o - dile, Nev - er

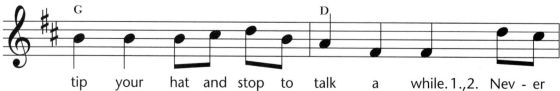

tip your hat and stop to talk a while. 1.,2. Nev - er

3. Don't be

Beware of Crocodile Moves!

Look at the Ⓐ and Ⓑ sections as you sing this song. Watch out for the **D.C. al Fine** at the end of the Ⓑ section. Where will you go next?

> **D.C. al Fine** is an Italian musical term that tells you to go back to the beginning of the song and sing until you see the word *Fine* [FEE-neh].

Make up a clapping game with a friend. Play it as you sing the song. Move to a new partner for each section.

run, walk a-way, say "Good-night," not "Good day!" Clear the
rude, nev-er mock, throw a kiss, not a rock.

aisle and nev-er smile at Mis-ter Croc-o-dile.

Ⓑ You may ve-ry well be well-bred,

Lots of et-i-quette in your head,

But there's al-ways some spe-cial case, time or

place to for-get et-i-quette.

Sing a Lullaby

This is a very old, well-known lullaby from Taiwan. Use the recorded Pronunciation Practice to learn to **sing** the song in Mandarin. Then **sing** it again in English.

3-17

Hwa yuan li-de young wa wa

(Garden Lullaby)

Words by Po-Yang Chou
English Words by Ellen Williams

Music by Chuen-Taur Su

妹 妹 背 著 洋 娃 娃 　 走 到 花 園 来 看 花
Mai mai bay ge young wa wa　jou dau hwa yuan lai kan hwa
Lit - tle sis - ter with her doll　Walks a-mong the gar-den walls.

娃 娃 哭 了 叫 媽 媽 　 樹 上 小 鳥 笑 哈 哈
wa wa koo le jau ma ma　shu shan siau niau siau ha ha.
"Ma - ma," cries the ba - by doll.　From the trees birds sing their calls.

Find the New Pitch

"Hwa yuan li-de young wa wa" contains these pitches that you can already **read.**

Listen to the song again. On which pitch does the song start? Find the place in the song where you hear a new pitch. Is it higher or lower than the pitches you already know?

Take a Step Down

The new pitch is even lower than low *la.* It is a step below low *la.*

so

mi

re

do

la

?

Music of Taiwan

Listen to this piece for solo piano. Try to hear the melody that repeats several times.

3-21
Lantern Festival

from *Taiwan Suite*
by Ma Shui-Long

Lantern Festival is about the celebration on the fifteenth day of the Chinese New Year.

Tune In

The piano has been used in Taiwan for more than 100 years. Many Taiwanese children take piano lessons.

M·U·S·I·C M·A·K·E·R·S

Ma Shui-Long

Ma Shui-Long (born 1939) is a well-known composer in Taiwan. He mixes traditional Taiwanese folk songs into his compositions. He writes music for orchestra, chamber ensemble, piano solo, vocal solo, and chorus. Ma has received many awards for his work. *Lantern Festival* is part of a collection of his piano pieces.

Arts Connection

The Beloved Grandchildren by Li Mei-Shu.
This painting shows the artist's grandchildren
in the mid-1900s. ▼

Meet the Artist

Li Mei-Shu (1902–1983) was interested in music
and painting from the time he was a child in
Taiwan. While going to school, he taught himself
to paint in his spare time. He later studied painting
in Japan, then returned to Taiwan to teach.
Li especially liked painting pictures of people.
His favorite subject was the Chinese people.

Web Site Visit *www.sbgmusic.com* to
learn more about Chinese and
Taiwanese music styles.

New Note Coming Through

There's a new pitch you can learn in this folk song from Alabama. **Listen** for the new pitch in the recording. Notice that the song starts on *do.*

3-22

Alabama Gal

Folk Song from Alabama

1. Come   through   'na   hur - ry,
2. I   don't   know   how,   how,

Come   through   'na   hur - ry,
I   don't   know   how,   how,

Come   through   'na   hur - ry,
I   don't   know   how,   how,

Al - a - bam - a   Gal.
Al - a - bam - a   Gal.

3. I showed you how, how, *(3 times)*
   Alabama Gal.

4. Ain't I rock candy, *(3 times)*
   Alabama Gal.

102

What's the Pitch Name?

The pitch that is a step lower than low *la* is called low *so*. You already know a hand sign for *so*. Can you guess what the hand sign is for low *so*?

Find the low *so* highlighted in the song. Then **sing** "Alabama Gal" with pitch syllables and hand signs.

Play-Party Time

Now it's time to learn the play-party, or dance, that goes with "Alabama Gal." **Move** like the children pictured below.

Wake Up and Sing

Sing "Never Sleep Late Any More."
Find the low *so* and low *la*.

3-24 Never Sleep Late Any More

Folk Song from the United States

1. Oh, just let me get up in the ear - ly morn,

Just let me get up in the ear - ly morn,

Just let me get up in the ear - ly morn, And I'll

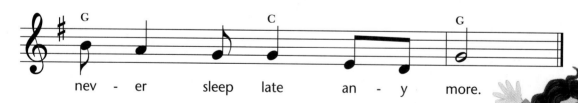

nev - er sleep late an - y more.

2. Oh, just let me stand up and walk around the world, . . .
   And I'll never sit down any more.

3. Oh, just let me shake hands with everyone I meet, . . .
   And I'll never shake hands any more.

4. Oh, just let me jump up like a jumping jack, . . .
   And I'll never jump up any more.

5. Oh, just let me bounce up like a rubber ball, . . .
   And I'll never sit down any more.

Monday!

by David L. Harrison

Overslept
Rain is pouring
Missed the bus
Dad is roaring
Late for school
Forgot my spelling
Soaking wet
Clothes are smelling
Dropped my books
Got them muddy
Flunked a test
Didn't study
Teacher says
I must do better
Lost my money
Tore my sweater
Feeling dumber
Feeling glummer
Monday sure can be
A bummer.

Show What You Know!

Find the pitches of this song on a xylophone. Then play the first line of "Never Sleep Late Any More."

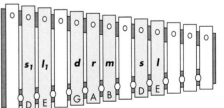

Add high *so* and *la.* Starting on *do,* **play** the scale first going up and then coming back down.

Sing the entire song using pitch syllables and hand signs. Try it with a partner. One person can sing and the other person can do the hand signs.

Welcome to the String Family

String instruments make sounds through vibration. The strings must be stretched across an open space, such as a box. The box amplifies, or makes louder, the sounds made by the vibrating string.

Try this experiment.

◄ Stretch a rubber band across the top of a box.

Pluck the rubber band to make it vibrate. ▶

How else could you make the rubber band vibrate?

Ways to Play

Here are two ways to play a string instrument.
Each way causes a string to vibrate.

◄ Plucking a string is like snapping the rubber band over the box.

◄ When bowing [BOH-ing], the player moves a bow across the strings.

 Video Library Learn more about string instruments from around the world in *String Instruments: Bowed* and *String Instruments: Plucked*

Meet the Players

Four string instruments have become a regular part of a large musical group called an orchestra. They are the violin, the viola, the cello [CHEL-oh], and the string bass [base].

What do you see about these instruments that is the same? What do you see that is different? Which instrument do you think plays the lowest sounds? Why?

Cello ▶

◀ String bass

String Tunes

Listen to this recording of a famous French melody.

- Hear the piece in **unison.**
- Hear the strings play **_arco_,** in a round.
- Hear the strings play **_pizzicato_,** on different parts.

3-25
Frère Jacques

**Traditional French
arranged by Buryl Red**

This melody has been sung around the world in many different languages.

Listen to *Winter*. Do you hear bowed or plucked strings?

3-26
Winter

**from *the Four Seasons*
by Antonio Vivaldi**

The four sections of this piece for string orchestra match the four seasons of the year.

Viola ▶

Describe the sounds you hear in this string quartet.

3-27
String Quartet No. 5

**Movement 4
by Béla Bartók**

The players use *pizzicato* and *arco* playing in this piece.

▼ Violin

SING GOOD MORNING!

Listen to "Had to Get Up This Mornin' Soon."
Then **sing** the song and snap your fingers to the
steady beat.

3-28

HAD TO GET UP THIS MORNIN' SOON

African American Song

A Em

Had to get up this morn - in' soon,

Had to get up this morn - in' soon,

Had to get up this morn - in' soon, soon,

Had to get up this morn - in' soon.

Morning Harmony

You have already played rhythmic ostinatos. Now you can learn a **melodic ostinato.** A melodic ostinato can be either sung or played on a pitched instrument.

A melody pattern that repeats several times is called a **melodic ostinato.**

Sing this melodic ostinato while the rest of the class sings the **A** section.

Up this morn - in' soon.

Did you know that any time after midnight is actually morning?

B

Em

1. Woke up this morn - in' in such big haste,
2. Got up this morn - in' an' got up so soon,

Bm   Em   D. C. al Fine

I did - n't have time to wash my face.
I could - n't see nothin' but the stars and moon.

Gathering Harmony

This song is sung in the musical play *Peter Pan* as the children are preparing for bed. What do you call this kind of song? **Listen** to "Tender Shepherd," and then **sing** the song.

3-30

Tender Shepherd

Words by Carolyn Leigh

Music by Mark Charlap

1. Ten - der shep - herd, ten - der shep - herd,
2. Ten - der shep - herd, ten - der shep - herd,

Watch - es o - ver all his sheep.
You for - got to count his sheep,

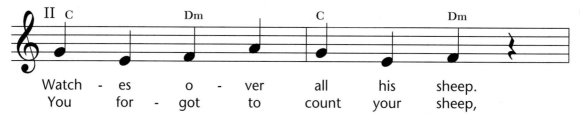

One, say your pray'rs, and two, close your eyes, And
One in the mead - ow, two in the gar - den,

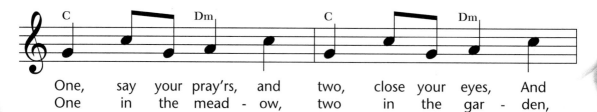

three, safe and hap - pi - ly fall a - sleep.
Three in the nur - ser - y fast a - sleep.

Play in Harmony

In the last lesson, you learned to sing a melodic ostinato. This time, you can **play** ostinatos that go with "Tender Shepherd."

Mary Martin

Mary Martin (1913–1990) began her career teaching dance, and singing on the radio, in her home state of Texas. She moved to New York to perform in several Broadway plays, then went to Hollywood to try movie acting. Martin starred in ten films. She returned to theater in 1949 and performed in many shows. Her most famous roles were the leads in *South Pacific* and *Peter Pan*.

Putting It

1. You're the composer, and you're making decisions about how you want your string quartet to sound.

   a. If you want the musicians to play so that the notes sound short or separated, tell them to play _____.
   1) *legato*   2) *staccato*

   b. If you want the musicians to play so that the notes sound connected and smooth, tell them to play _____.
   1) *legato*   2) *staccato*

   c. If you want the music to sound *staccato*, ask them to play _____.
   1) *arco*   2) *pizzicato*

   d. For *legato* sounds, ask them to play _____.
   1) *arco*   2) *pizzicato*

2. Read these rhythms. Which ones last for one beat?

   a. ♩   **b.** ♩   **c.** ♫♫   **d.** 𝄽   **e.** ♫

You will hear three examples of string instruments.
Point to the word that matches the instrument you hear.
Is the instrument played *arco* or *pizzicato?*

1. string bass   viola
2. string bass   piano
3. cello   violin

All Together

Move with the Music

Listen to the recording of *Gavotte* on page 84. Move to match each section of the piece. Use short movements for the *staccato* sections, and smoother movements for the *legato* section.

Create an Ostinato

Create a simple rhythm ostinato to accompany *"Hwa yuan li-de young wa wa"* on page 98.

• Choose from these rhythms for your four-beat ostinato.

• Perform your ostinato softly using body percussion as you sing.

• Then perform your ostinato on unpitched percussion instruments. Choose instruments with timbres that match the song.

Improvise a Melody

Improvise a melody for your rhythm ostinato. Use these pitches. Begin and end on F or C.

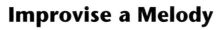

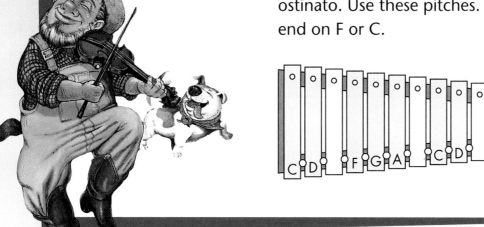

Rhythm Skill Builder

Here's a way to practice your rhythm skills and get on your feet! Choose a line of this speech piece to learn. Put your part together with classmates to **perform** this famous tongue-twister.

3-35

How Much Wood Could a Woodchuck Chuck

Setting by Grace Nash

Building Our Musical Skills

Singing the Blues

There is a legend about Groundhog Day. If a groundhog sees its shadow on February 2, there will be six more weeks of winter. If not, spring will come early.

Sing "The Groundhog Blues." What happens?

The Groundhog Blues

3-37

Words and Music by Gayle Giese

With a swing

The ground-hog crept right out of the log, ___

The sun shone down, bright on that hog. ___

The ground-hog was a hog of small brain, ___

He did not know his Sha-dow by name. ___

Hog met Sha-dow and said in fright, ___

Did you know that another name for a woodchuck is "groundhog"?

"Whoa! Back to my log, I'm out of this light!"

'Twas a ver-y sad thing that hog was so meek,

For win-ter roared for six ___ more weeks!

Repeat 2 times

I've got the ground-hog blues; it's win-ter, it's cold!

I've got the ground - hog ___ blues. Brrrrr!

119

Moving Fast and Slow

Before pipes were installed to bring water into houses, people got water from wells in the ground. To "draw" a bucket of water meant to pull the bucket up out of the well.

Listen for a tempo change as you **sing** the song.

 3-39

Draw Me a Bucket of Water

African American Singing Game

Moderato

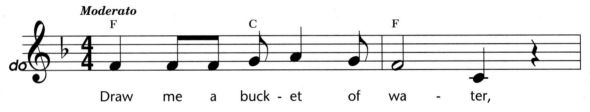

Draw   me   a   buck - et   of   wa   -   ter,

For   my   old - est   daugh   -   ter,

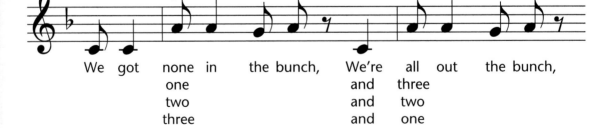

We	got	none	in	the bunch,	We're	all	out	the bunch,
		one				and	three	
		two				and	two	
		three				and	one	

You   go   un - der   sis - ter   Sal   -   ly.

Repeat 3 times

Hurry Up!

You know that tempo is the speed of the beat. In the recording of "Draw Me a Bucket of Water," you hear a **subito** tempo change between the two sections of the song. Does the music get faster or slower?

Subito means "sudden."

Allegro

Frog in the buck - et and I can't get him out,

Frog in the buck - et and I can't get him out,

Frog in the buck - et and I can't get him out,

Repeat 1 time

Frog in the buck - et and I can't get him out.

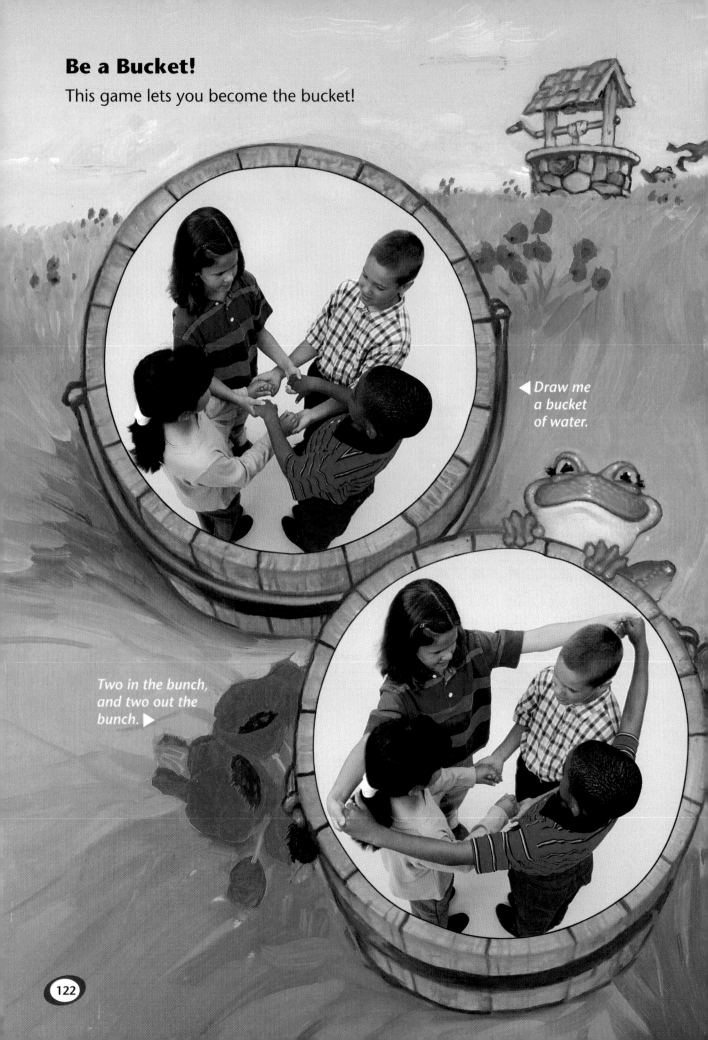

Be a Bucket!

This game lets you become the bucket!

◀ *Draw me a bucket of water.*

Two in the bunch, and two out the bunch. ▶

Frog in the bucket and I can't get him out.

Listen to this orchestral piece by an African American composer. Does the tempo change or stay the same?

4–1
Ennanga, Movement III

by William Grant Still

Ennanga is the name of a zither from Uganda, a country in Africa.

Sing with Strong Beats

"Morning Is Come" is a perfect way to wake up your voice. **Listen** to "Morning Is Come." Then **sing** the song.

Morning Is Come

Round from England

Morn - ing is come, night is a - way,

Rise with the sun _____ and _ wel - come the day.

How many beats are in each group of birds below?
Tap the beats as you **sing** the song again.

Groups of Three

This song moves in a pattern of three beats, one strong beat and two weak beats.

Create your own motions to show this pattern of strong and weak beats. Be sure the first beat feels strong!

One Sound, Three Beats

You already know this two-beat note. ♩

You also know this one-beat note. ♩

These notes tied together last for three beats. It can be written like this. ♩‿♩

It can also be written like this. ♩.

Find the ♩. in the music. Then **sing** the song while you do a pat-clap-clap pattern.

Beats and Bar Lines

Follow the rhythms below as you **listen** to "The Juniper Tree." Look for the note that gets three beats. What looks different about this music?

Oh, sis - ter Phoe - be, how mer - ry were we, The

night we sat un - der the jun - i - per tree, The

jun - i - per tree, hi - o, hi - o, The

jun - i - per tree, hi - o.

Tune In

Juniper trees can be as short as shrubs and as tall as giant cypress trees.

Add the Bar Lines

Bar lines are drawn to show how beats are grouped together in music. The space between two bar lines is called a **measure.** The number "3" at the beginning of this song shows that there are three beats in each measure. A **double bar line** means you have reached the end of the song.

Sing "The Juniper Tree" and look for the bar lines.

The Juniper Tree

Folk Song from Arkansas

1. Oh, sis - ter Phoe - be, how mer - ry were we, The
2. Go choose a part - ner, so choose you a one, Go

night we sat un - der the jun - i - per tree, The
choose you the fair - est that ev - er you can. Now

jun - i - per tree, hi - o, hi - o, The
rise you up, gal, and go, and go, Now

jun - i - per tree, hi - o.
rise you up, gal, and go.

Copyright by John A. Lomax, 1937.

Enjoying Rhythm

Think about the place where you live. What do you like best? **Listen** to *"¡Qué gusto!"* What does the singer like about living in the country?

4-6

¡Qué gusto!
(What Pleasure)

English Words by Ruth DeCesare and Ellen Traeger   *Hispanic Song of the American Southwest*

¡Qué gus - to,   qué gus - to,   qué gus - to   me   da,
What pleas - ure,   what plea - sure   and   joy   it   gives   me

vi - vir   en   el   cam - po   con   tran - qui - li - dad!
to   live   in   the   coun - try,   so   peace - ful   and   free!

Yo   can - to,   yo   brin - co   a   mi   li - ber - tad,
I   sing   and   I   dance   and   I   jump   all   a - round,

por - que   no   hay   ti - je - ras   de   la   so - cie - dad.
ver - y   free   of   the   crowds   and   the   noise   I   once found.

Move to the Country

Look at the beginning of the song. What do you see before the first bar line? This note is called the **upbeat. Sing** the song and **move** to show the upbeat.

> An **upbeat** is one or more notes before the first strong beat of a phrase.

Si me pongo yo a cantar

Translated by Joseph F. Domínguez

If I begin to sing
For a whole year long
Not once will I be heard
Repeating the same song.

*Si me pongo yo a cantar
Un año y sus doce meses,
No me han de sentir enchar
La misma cancion dos veces.*

Show What You Know!

Practice saying the rhythms below with rhythm syllables. Then **perform** them with two classmates. Which of these rhythms has an upbeat? Be ready to explain your answer.

1.

2.

3.

Around and AROUND and Around

Listen to "*Doong gul ge,*" a Korean singing game. It has two sections, **A** and **B**, but you sing the **A** section twice. This is called **A** **B** **A** form.

4-10

Doong gul ge

('Round and Around We Go)

English Words by Kim Williams   *Korean Words and Music by Lee Su In*

둥 글 게 둥 글 게 (손뼉) 둥 글 게 둥 글 게 (손뼉)
Doong gul ge doong gul ge,   *doong gul ge doong gul ge,*
'Round and a-round we go,   'round and a-round we go!

빙 글 빙 글 돌 아 가 며 춤 을 춥 시 다 (손뼉)
bing gul bing gul dol ah kah miaw chum ul chup shi da.
Dance a-round the cir - cle now, don't let your feet be slow.

손 뼉 을 치 면 서 (손뼉) 노 래 를 부 르 며 (손뼉)
Son bia kul chi mian sawh,   *no reh rul pu ru miaw,*
Cir-cle a-round and clap,   cir-cle a-round and sing,

랄 랄 랄 라 즐 거 웁 게 춤 추 자
la la la la chul kaw up ge chum chu cha.
Let's all run to-geth - er now a-round the ring!

China

Korean Peninsula ▶

Tune In

North Korea and South Korea are on a peninsula. A peninsula is land surrounded by water on three sides.

링 가 링 가 링   가 링 가 링 가 링
Ring - a - ring - a - ring   a - ring - a - ring - a - ring,
Ring - a - ring - a - ring   a - ring - a - ring - a - ring,

링 가 링 가 링   가 링 가 링 가 링
ring - a - ring - a - ring   a - ring - a - ring - a - ring.
ring - a - ring - a - ring   a - ring - a - ring - a - ring.

손 에 손 을 잡   고 모 두 다 함 께
Son eh son ul cho(p)   go mo du da hahm ge,
Hop - ping as   we go   and jump - ing as   we sing,

D.C. al Fine

즐 거 웁 게 춤 을 춥   시 다 _____
chul kaw up ge chum ul chup   shi da. _____
Let's   all   run   to - geth - er 'round   the   ring! _____

Move Around

Learn to play a singing game that goes with "*Doong gul ge.*"

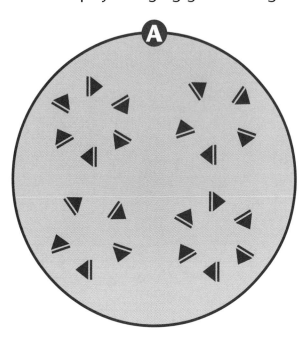

A Walk in small circles. Change direction whenever you hear hand claps in the music. Clap your hands too!

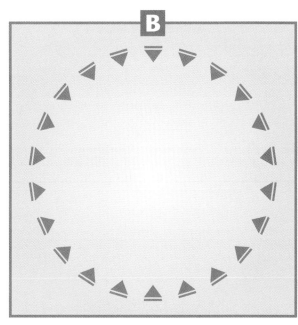

B Join in a big circle. Jump in and out when you hear "*Son eh son ul chop*" or "Hopping as we go."

Arts Connection

◀ This porcelain jar with iron-brown underglaze was made in Korea in the 1700s.

Music of Korea

The *kayagum* [kah-YAH-guhm] is a Korean folk instrument. The term *kayagum pyongch'ang* describes a person playing the *kayagum* and singing with his or her instrument.

Listen to this traditional Korean music.

4-14
Kayagum pyongch'ang-sae t'aryug

Traditional Korean

This piece is an example of Korean music, which has four thousand years of tradition.

kayagum
▼

Forms of Morning

Roosters crow before the day begins. What sounds wake you up in the morning? **Listen** for the **introduction** and **coda** in "*Kum bachur atzel.*"

> An **introduction** is music that is played before the words are sung.

> A **coda** is music that ends a song after the words are sung.

4-15

Kum bachur atzel
(Hear the Rooster Crowing)

English Words by David ben Avraham

Folk Song from Israel

Kum ba - chur a - tzel___ v' - tzei la - a - vo - da,
Hear the roost - er crow - ing, A - crow - ing at the dawn;

Kum ba - chur a - tzel___ v' - tzei la - a - vo - da;
Hear the roost - er crow - ing, A - crow - ing at the dawn.

Kum, kum,___ v' - tzei la - a - vo - da.
Wake, wake,___ for now the night has gone;

Kum, kum,___ v' - tzei la - a - vo - da.
Wake, wake,___ for now the night has gone.

Play with the Rooster

Create a new introduction and coda for this song. Use instruments that make morning sounds. **Play** your music.

Then **play** this accompaniment for *"Kum bachur atzel."*

More Music from Israel

Now **listen** to *Tzlil Zugim*. Notice the introduction, and **listen** for the coda at the end.

4-18
Tzlil Zugim

Traditional from Israel

This song is often performed for dancing.

Ku - ku - ri - ku,   ku - ku - ri - ku,   tar - n' - gol   ka - ra;
Ku - ku - ri - ku,   ku - ku - ri - ku,   yawn   a might - y   yawn;

Ku - ku - ri - ku,   ku - ku - ri - ku,   tar - n' - gol   ka - ra.
Ku - ku - ri - ku,   ku - ku - ri - ku,   yawn   a might - y   yawn.

New Pitch in the House

"Li'l Liza Jane" is a verse and refrain song from the United States. **Listen** for a new pitch in "Li'l Liza Jane."

4-19

Li'l Liza Jane

Dance Song from the United States

VERSE

1. I got a house in Bal - ti - more, Li'l Li - za Jane,
2. I got a house in Bal - ti - more, Li'l Li - za Jane,

Street-car runs right by my door, Li'l Li - za Jane.
Brus - sels car - pet on the floor, Li'l Li - za Jane.

Start on a High Note

The refrain of "Li'l Liza Jane" begins with a new pitch. Does it sound higher or lower than the pitches in the verse?

The new pitch is called *do'*, just like the *do* you already know. What is different about this pitch?

do   re   mi   so   la   do'

Now **sing** the refrain with pitch syllables and hand signs. You already know the hand sign for the new pitch!

REFRAIN

Oh,   E - li - za,   Li'l   Li - za   Jane,

Oh,   E - li - za,   Li'l   Li - za   Jane.

3. I got a house in Baltimore,
   Li'l Liza Jane,
   Silver doorplate on the door,
   Li'l Liza Jane.

4. Come, my love, and be with me,
   Li'l Liza Jane,
   And I'll take good care of thee,
   Li'l Liza Jane.

Hop Up to a High Note

This is a song from the days before automobiles! **Listen** to discover how many ladies fit in the buggy. Then **sing** the song.

4-21

Hop Up, My Ladies

Folk Song from the United States

VERSE   D   G   D

1. Did you e - ver go to meet-ing, Un - cle Joe, Un - cle Joe?

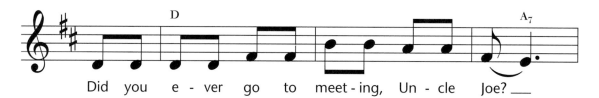

D   A₇

Did you e - ver go to meet - ing, Un - cle Joe? ___

D   G   D

Did you e - ver go to meet-ing, Un - cle Joe, Un - cle Joe?

G   D   A₇   D

I don't mind the weath-er, if the wind don't blow.

From *do* to High *do*

Sing these pitches with hand signs and pitch syllables. Point to high *do*.

do   re   mi   so   la   do'

Now **sing** the refrain of the song with pitch syllables. Notice the leap from *do* to high *do*. The distance from *do* to high *do* is called an **octave.**

> An **octave** is the distance between one note and the next higher or lower note that has the same name.

REFRAIN

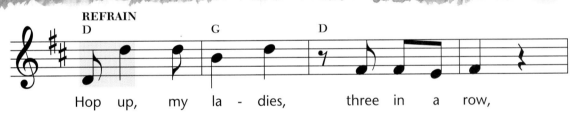

Hop up, my la - dies, three in a row,

Hop up, my la - dies, three in a row,

Hop up, my la - dies, three in a row,

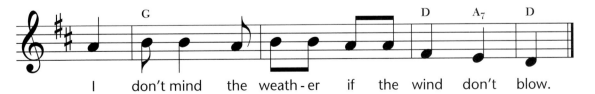

I don't mind the weath-er if the wind don't blow.

2. Will your horse carry double,
   Uncle Joe, Uncle Joe? . . .
   Refrain

3. Is your horse a single footer,
   Uncle Joe, Uncle Joe? . . .
   Refrain

Music from the Movies

Listen to the very beginning of this piece to hear the first octave leap. It goes by quickly! Then **listen** for high *do* in the theme shown below.

4–23
The Magnificent Seven

by Elmer Bernstein

The Magnificent Seven is an American western movie from 1960. This piece from the movie score is one of Bernstein's best-known works.

The Magnificent Seven
Listening Map

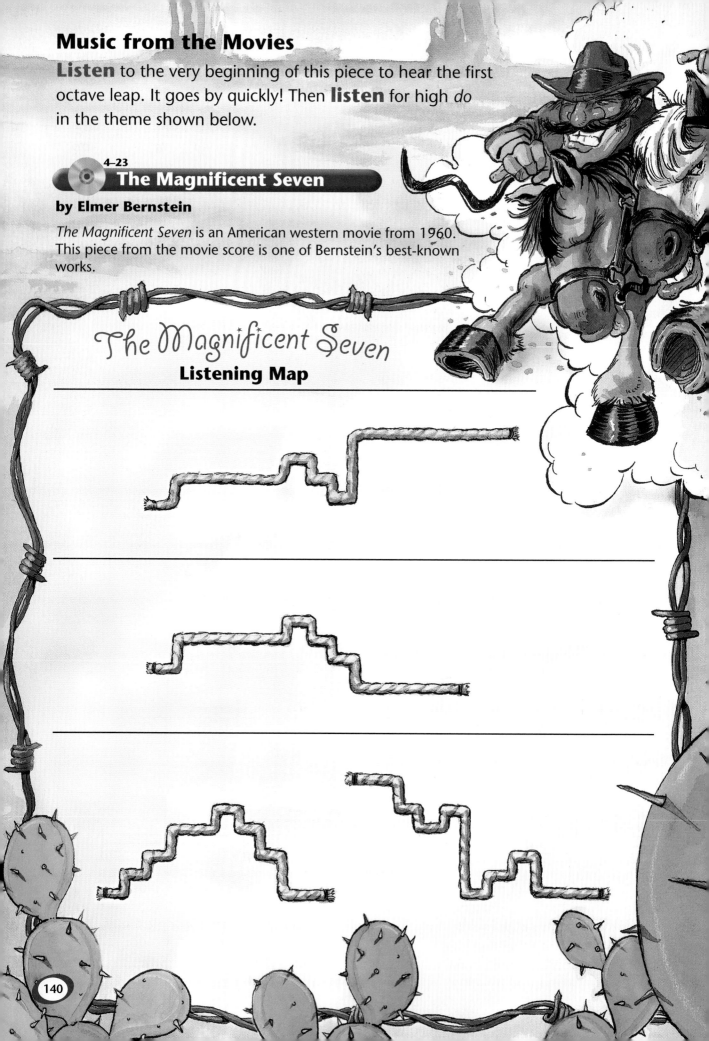

The *Magnificent Seven* was one of many western movies released in the United States in the 1960s and 1970s. Each movie had its own unique musical score.

M·U·S·I·C M·A·K·E·R·S

Elmer Bernstein

Elmer Bernstein (born 1922) has written the music for many movies over the last 40 years. He graduated from The Juilliard School of Music in New York. His first major movie score was the Frank Sinatra movie, *The Man with the Golden Arm.* He also wrote the music for *Ghostbusters* and *To Kill a Mockingbird.* His music mixes American classical style with jazz.

Web Site Go to *www.sbgmusic.com* to learn more about music for the movies.

Sing and Play Together

"Walk Together, Children" is a spiritual in which you sing high *do*. **Listen** to the song. The first note of the song is *so*. The last note of the song is *do*. Where is high *do*?

 4-24

Walk Together, Children

African American Spiritual

1. Oh, walk to-geth-er, chil-dren, Don't you get __ wea - ry,
2. Oh, talk to-geth-er, chil-dren, Don't you get __ wea - ry,

Walk to-geth-er, chil-dren, Don't you get wea - ry,
Talk to-geth-er, chil-dren, Don't you get wea - ry,

Oh, walk to-geth-er, chil-dren, Don't you get __ wea - ry,
Oh, talk to-geth-er, chil-dren, Don't you get __ wea - ry,

There's a great camp-meet-ing in the prom-ised land.
There's a great camp-meet-ing in the prom-ised land.

3. Oh, sing together, children, . . .   4. Oh, shout together, children, . . .

Create and Play

Create percussion ostinatos to accompany this song. Make up a different ostinato for each verse.

Now add this melodic ostinato that includes both high and low *do.* **Play** it on a keyboard or bells.

(Repeat 6 times)

Show What You Know!

1. Here are all of the pitches you know. **Sing** from *do* to high *do* and back again.

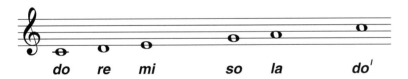

2. Where is high *do?* For each *do,* point to the place on the staff where you would expect to find high *do.* Use the first example as a guide.

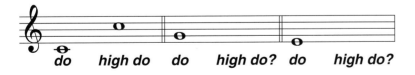

3. Look back! Find the high *do* in either "Li'l Liza Jane," on page 136 or "Hop Up, My Ladies," on page 138. **Sing** the phrases that include high *do* using pitch syllables.

Mallet Magic

Some percussion instruments have bars arranged like a piano keyboard. The bars are played with mallets. Mallets are sticks with rubber, felt, wood, or yarn balls on one end.

Meet the Xylophone

The xylophone is one of the oldest mallet instruments. *Xylophone* means "wood sound." The bars of a xylophone are made out of wood.

▼ xylophone (orchestral)

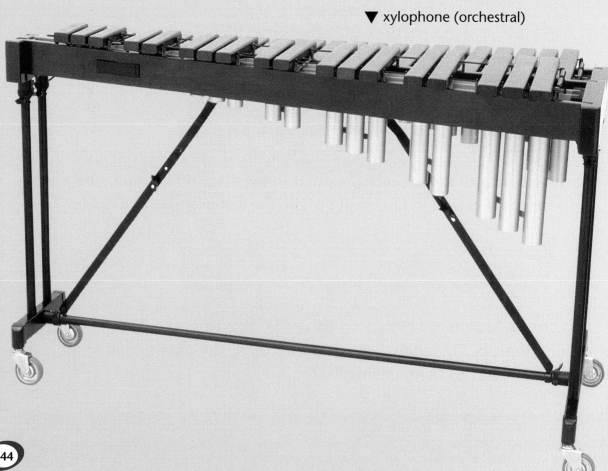

Xylophone Sound

Listen to this xylophone solo played by Evelyn Glennie.

4-26
Whirlwind

by Joe Green

A brass band plays the accompaniment in this recording.

MUSIC MAKERS
Evelyn Glennie

Evelyn Glennie (born 1965) was born in Aberdeen, Scotland. When she was twelve years old, she began playing percussion instruments. Now she performs with musicians in many countries and from many cultures. Glennie is one of only a few female solo percussionists in the world.

Video Library See an eight-year-old play mallet instruments in *Percussion Instruments: Tuned.*

Marimba Magic

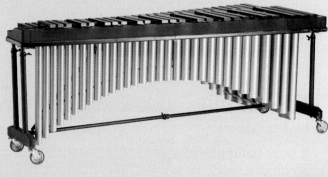

▼ marimba (orchestral)

The marimba is similar to the xylophone, but it has long resonating tubes that hang below each bar. The marimba has a more mellow sound than the xylophone.

Listen to *Memories of the Seashore*, played by Keiko Abe [KAY-ko AH-bay]. How would you **describe** a marimba's sound?

4-27

Memories of the Seashore

Written and performed by Keiko Abe

Abe imagined the ocean as she wrote this piece.

M·U·S·I·C M·A·K·E·R·S

Keiko Abe

Keiko Abe (born 1937) is a Japanese marimba virtuoso, composer, teacher, and music arranger for percussion. She was born in Tokyo and played piano and xylophone as a child. She began composing at a young age. She chose the marimba as her main instrument when she was twelve years old. Abe also designs marimbas. She was one of Evelyn Glennie's teachers.

Lionel Hampton

Lionel Hampton (born 1913) was born in Louisville, Kentucky. He joined a drum and bugle corps as a boy. As he got older, he played in jazz groups and learned the marimba. Jazz trumpeter Louis Armstrong encouraged Hampton to try the vibraphone, or "vibes." Soon Hampton formed his own band, featuring the vibes. Lionel Hampton's band was one of the most famous of the swing era.

More Magic

The vibraphone has metal bars and a resonating tube below each bar. A small, electric motor in the tube spins a metal fan when a switch is turned on. The spinning fan makes the vibrating sound.

Listen to Lionel Hampton play the vibraphone in the jazz composition *Pick-a-Rib.*

4-28
Pick-a-Rib

by Goodman and Hampton

The vibraphone has been used in many kinds of ensembles. It was a very popular instrument in the early days of jazz.

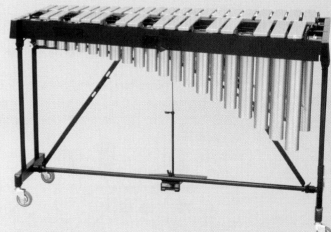

Partner Songs

Here is a song you may already know. **Sing** "This Old Man." Get ready for a special challenge!

 4-29

This Old Man

Folk Song from England

1. This old man, he played one, He played nick-nack on my drum.
2. This old man, he played two, He played nick-nack on my shoe.

Nick-nack pad-dy-whack, give the dog a bone. This old man came roll-ing home.

3. . . . three, He played nick-nack on my tree.

4. . . . four, He played nick-nack on my door.

5. . . . five, He played nick-nack on my hive.

6. . . . six, He played nick-nack on my sticks.

7. . . . seven, He played nick-nack on my oven.

8. . . . eight, He played nick-nack on my gate.

9. . . . nine, He played nick-nack on my line.

10. . . . ten, He played nick-nack on my hen.

Begin a New Song

Now learn a new song. **Listen** for the nonsense words in "Michael Finnigan," then **sing** along.

4-31

Michael Finnigan

Traditional from the United States

1. There was an old man named Mi - chael Fin - ni - gan,
2. There was an old man named Mi - chael Fin - ni - gan,
3. There was an old man named Mi - chael Fin - ni - gan,

He had whis - kers on his chin - ni - gan, The
He went fish - ing with a pin - ni - gan, He
Climbed a tree and barked his shin - ni - gan, He

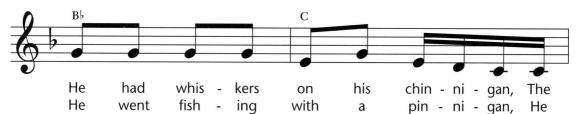

wind came up and blew them in a - gain,
caught a fish but dropped it in a - gain,
lost a - bout a yard of skin - ni - gan,

Poor old Mi - chael Fin - ni - gan. Be - gin a - gain.

4. There was an old man named Michael Finnigan,
   He grew fat and then grew thinnigan,
   Then he died and had to begin again,
   Poor old Michael Finnigan. Begin again.

A Special Challenge!

Sing "This Old Man" and "Michael Finnigan" as partner songs. **Sing** one song with half of your class while the rest of the class sings the other song.

One Song, Two Melodies

Plants need sun and rain to grow. What do you need to grow?

Sing "Each of Us Is a Flower."

4-34

Each of Us Is a Flower

Words and Music by Charlotte Diamond

Each of us ___ is a flow - er,

Grow - ing in ___ life's ___ gar - den. ___

Each of us ___ is a flow - er,

We need ___ the sun ___ and rain.

Making Beautiful Music

"Each of Us Is a Flower" can be sung as a partner
song with itself. Sing the first melody Ⓐ. Then practice
the second melody Ⓑ. Then sing the two melodies at the
same time to form a partner song.

Sun, _____ shine your warmth on ___ me.

Moon, _____ cool me with your _ night.

Wind, _____ bring the gen - tle ___ rain.

Earth, _____ dig my roots down deep.

1. Look at the notation for "Hop Up, My Ladies" on page 138.

    a. Point to two places in the song where each of the following pitches occurs.

        so   la   mi   re   high do

    b. Point to a bar line in the music.

    c. Point to the double bar line.

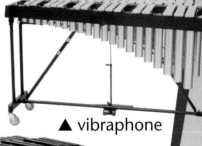

2. *Subito* means

    a. fast   **b.** sudden   **c.** gradual

3. Look at the photographs below.

    a. Point to the instruments with bars made of wood.

    b. Point to the instrument with bars made of metal.

4-36

What Do You Hear? 4

You will hear three different mallet instruments. Point to the word that matches the instrument you hear.

    1. xylophone   marimba   vibraphone

    2. xylophone   marimba   vibraphone

    3. xylophone   marimba   vibraphone

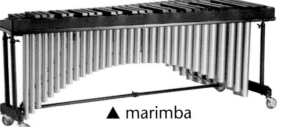

▲ vibraphone

▲ xylophone   ▲ marimba

All Together

Sing a Partner Song

Sing "Each of Us is a Flower" on page 150. Everyone sings the **A** section followed by the **B** section.

- Then sing both sections at the same time, with a different group singing each section.

- Always sing with good vocal quality.

- Make sure that both melodies are heard when they are sung together.

Create Music

Create an introduction and a coda for "Each of Us Is a Flower."

- Choose a rhythm pattern from the song to use in your introduction and coda.

- What instruments will you use to match the style of the song?

Jazz It Up!

Jazz has been a part of our music for almost one hundred years. It was made famous by musicians like Louis Armstrong, Ella Fitzgerald, and Sarah Vaughan.

One style of jazz singing is called **scat.** It may have been created by Louis Armstrong when he forgot the words to a song while performing.

Scat is a style of jazz singing where nonsense syllables take the place of words.

Learn to Scat

Listen to *Alphabet Scat.* Sing along when you can.

4-39
Alphabet Scat

by Lisa Yves

This composer has written many jazz pieces for children.

Listen to this famous jazz piece using scat.

4-40
Lullaby of Birdland

**by George Shearing
as sung by Sarah Vaughan**

This jazz song has been recorded by many artists.

Discovering New Musical Horizons

M·U·S·I·C   M·A·K·E·R·S

Sarah Vaughan

Sarah Vaughan (1924–1990) was one of the great jazz singers. She sang with almost every major jazz band of her time, and at the White House in Washington, D.C.

Vaughan began studying piano and organ at age seven. When she was sixteen, she entered and won a talent contest at the Apollo Theater in Harlem in New York City. Her professional career took her all over the world. She created many memorable recordings.

Mix It Up!

The composers of "Cement Mixer" liked to add nonsense words to their songs. It was their own version of scat.

Count how many times you hear nonsense words as you **listen** to this song.

Cement Mixer

4-41

Words and Music by Slim Gaillard and Lee Ricks

Ce - ment   mix - er!   put - ti,   put - ti,

Ce - ment   mix - er!   put - ti,   put - ti,

Last Time to Coda

Ce - ment   mix - er!   put - ti,   put - ti,

A   pud-dle o' voot - y,   pud-dle o' goot - y,   pud-dle o' scoot - y.

2.

A pud-dle o' veet, Con - crete.

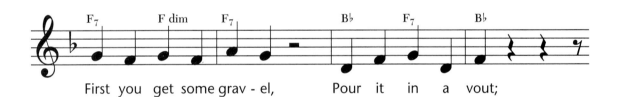

First you get some grav - el, Pour it in a vout;

To mix a mess o' mor - tar, you add ce - ment and wa - ter.

D. C. al Coda

See the mel - low roon - y come out, __ slurp, slurp, slurp.

Who wants a buck - et of ce - ment?

Dynamic Choices

How do you decide how loudly or how softly to sing a song? Look for clues in the words of this song that tell you what dynamics you might choose.

5-1

Hush, Hush

African American Spiritual

1. Hush,   hush,   some- bod-y's call-in' my name,
2. Who,   who,   who, Lord, is call-in' my name?

Hush,   hush,   some- bod-y's call-in' my   name, _____
Who,   who,   who, Lord, is call-in' my   name? _____

Hush,   hush,   some- bod-y's call-in' my name,
Who,   who,   who, Lord,   is call-in' my name?

Oh, my Lord, _   oh, my Lord, _ what shall I   do? ___
Oh, my Lord, _   oh, my Lord, _ what shall I   do? ___

3. You, you, you, Lord, are callin' my name, . . .

Singing Sounds

Listen to this piece. How would you describe the dynamics in this song?

Alleluia

from _Mass for the 21st Century_
by Carman Moore

This work was recorded live in New York City.

Meet the Composer

Listen to Carman Moore discuss his work.

Interview with Carman Moore

M·U·S·I·C M·A·K·E·R·S

Carman Moore

Carman Moore (born 1936) is from Ohio. He studied French horn, cello, and music history at The Ohio State University. Later he moved to New York City, where he studied composition at The Juilliard School of Music. His compositions include works for orchestra, opera, theater, dance, and film.

The _Mass for the 21st Century_ was written for and performed at Lincoln Center in New York City. It has also been performed in South Africa, Australia, and Japan.

MIDI Change the dynamics in the MIDI song file for "Hush, Hush."

Show Some Spirit!

"Do, Lord" has two sections, a verse and a refrain. Which section is repeated? How are the dynamics in this song different from "Hush, Hush"?

Play this accompaniment on the refrain of "Do, Lord."

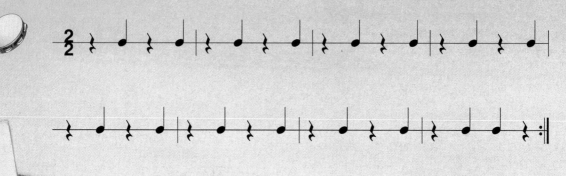

5-5

Do, Lord

African American Spiritual

REFRAIN

Do, Lord,   oh   do, Lord,   oh   do   re-mem-ber   me,

Do, Lord,   oh   do, Lord,   oh   do   re-mem-ber   me.

Do, Lord,   oh   do, Lord,   oh   do   re-mem-ber   me,

Ritard last time

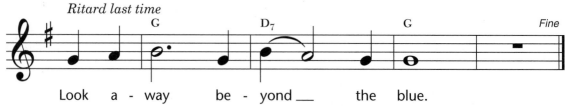

Look   a - way   be - yond ___   the   blue.

160

Add a Part

Play this accompaniment on the verse of the song.

I got a home in glo-ry land that out-shines the sun,

I got a home in glo-ry land that out-shines the sun.

I got a home in glo-ry land that out-shines the sun,

Look a-way be-yond ___ the blue.

Working Rhythms

Before machines were invented to do heavy labor, these jobs were done by large groups of workers. Why would they not want the captain's watch to run down and stop?

Listen for different rhythms as you **sing** the song.

 5-7

Don't Let Your Watch Run Down

Work Song from South Texas

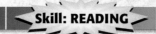

Don't let your watch run down, Cap-tain,

Don't let your watch run down. _____

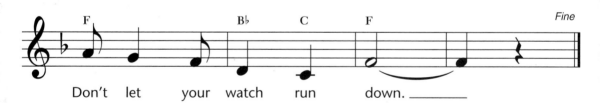

1. Wor-kin' on the lev - ee, dol-lar and a half a day,

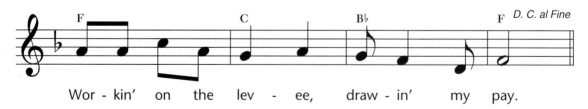

Wor-kin' on the lev - ee, draw-in' my pay.

2. Workin' on the railroad, mud up to my knees,
   Workin' on the railroad, tryin' to please. *Refrain*

3. When you see me comin', hoist your window high,
   When you see me leavin', bow down and cry. *Refrain*

Rhythms to Read

This song has rhythm patterns you know. Find each rhythm that lasts for one beat. Then find each pattern that lasts for two beats. Where is the pattern that lasts for three beats? HINT: Look for a tie.

Show What You Know!

Say the rhythms below, using rhythm syllables. How many beats are in each train car?

Frontier Rhythms

In the frontier days of America, people danced for entertainment. Going to a dance was a way to meet neighbors and relax. Here's a frontier song you can still dance to today. **Listen** to "Coffee Grows on White Oak Trees."

5-8

Coffee Grows on White Oak Trees

Folk Song from the United States

REFRAIN

Cof - fee grows on white oak trees.

The riv - er flows with hon - ey - o.

Go choose some - one to roam with you,

As sweet as m'las - ses can - dy - o.

Two or Three?

Which section of this song is written in meter in 3? Which section is in meter in 2?

Partners in Rhythm

Pick a partner and choose two different instruments. As you **sing** this song, **play** on the first beat of each measure. Your partner then plays the other beat or beats in the measure on his or her instrument.

VERSE

1. Two in the mid - dle and they can't go o - ver,

Two in the mid - dle and they can't go o - ver,

Two in the mid - dle and they can't go o - ver,

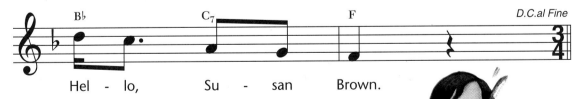

Hel - lo, Su - san Brown.

2. Swing you another one and you'll get over, *(3 times)*
   Hello, Susan Brown. *Refrain*

3. Four in the middle and they all go over, *(3 times)*
   Hello, Susan Brown. *Refrain*

LESSON 4

| Element: RHYTHM | Skill: MOVING | Connection: SCIENCE |

Waltzing Bear Rhythms

Caution! Bears Dancing

This comical song is about someone who likes to waltz with bears. What is the meter of the song? Follow the paw prints on the edge of the page with your finger as you **listen** to the recording. Why are some of the paw prints bigger than others?

5-10

Waltzing with Bears

Words and Music by Dale Marxen

REFRAIN

He goes wa - wa - wa - wa - wa, waltz - ing with bears,

Rag - gy bears, bag - gy bears, shag - gy bears, too.

There's noth - ing on earth Un - cle Wal - ter won't do

So he can go waltz - ing, wa - wa - wa - waltz - ing,

So he can go waltz - ing, waltz - ing with bears.

VERSE

1. I went to his room in the mid-dle of the night,

I tip-toed in-side and turned on the light,

Last verse to Coda

But to my dis-may, he was no-where in sight,

To Refrain

My un-cle Wal-ter goes waltz-ing at night.

Coda
(Freely)

Now he's waltz-ing with pan-das, and we don't un-der-stand it,

To Refrain

But the bears all de-mand at least one waltz a day!

2. We bought Uncle Walter a new coat to wear,
   But when he comes home it's all covered with hair,
   And lately I've noticed there are several new tears,
   My uncle Walter goes waltzing with bears.   *Refrain*

3. We told Uncle Walter that he should be good,
   And do all the things we say that he should,
   But I know that he'd rather be off in the woods,
   We're afraid we will lose him, we'll lose him for good.   *Refrain*

4. We said, "Uncle Walter, oh, please won't you stay,"
   And managed to keep him at home for a day,
   But the bears all barged in and they took him away.   *(to Coda)*

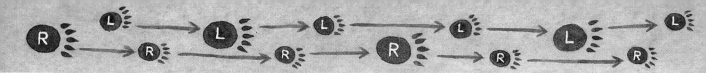

Listen to a Bear Dance

Listen to this piece by Béla Bartók and tap the beats on the listening map. What is the meter of this piece?

5-12
Bear Dance

**from *Ten Easy Pieces*
by Béla Bartók**

Bartók wrote this piece to help students learn to play the piano.

Bear Dance
Listening Map

(continues)

ending (1:36)

 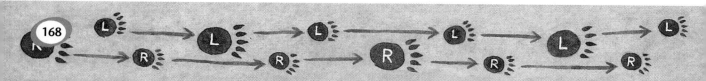

M·U·S·I·C M·A·K·E·R·S

Béla Bartók

Béla Bartók (1881–1945) is Hungary's most famous composer. He studied piano and composition at the Royal Academy in Budapest. In the early 1900s he traveled around Hungary listening to folk songs. He included many of these melodies and rhythms in his compositions. The *Ten Easy Pieces* are all based on folk melodies and folk rhythms.

Waltz Like a Bear

Imagine that you are a bear in "Waltzing with Bears." Stand on your hind legs and take a heavy step with your right foot. Then lightly step left-right. Repeat, beginning with your left foot. Hold up your front paws and sway!

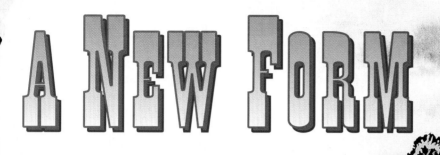

A New Form

Listen to discover the form of this song.

Railroad Corral

5-13

Cowboy Song from the United States

A G C

1. We're up in the morn - ing 'ere break - ing of day,
2. Come take up your cin - ches, come shake out your reins,

D G

The chuck wag - on's bus - y, the flap - jacks in play;
Come wake your old bron - co and break for the plains.

A G C

The herds are a - stir ov - er hill - side and dale
Come rout out your steer from the long chap - ar - ral,

D G

The night rid - ers push - ing them on to the trail.
The out - fit is off to the rail - road cor - ral.

Cowhand Talk

railroad corral — a railroad station from which cattle are shipped to market

chuck wagon — a portable kitchen on a cart

cinch — a strap used to hold a saddle on a horse

rawhide — a whip made of untanned cowhide

chaparral — a thicket of shrubs and thorny bushes

bronco — a wild horse found in the western United States

In the 1800s cowhands were usually men, but today both men and women work as cowhands.

Whoo-pi – ti – yi – ay, whoo-pi – ti – yi – ay!

Swing out your raw - hides and give them full play.

We're up in the morn - ing 'ere break - ing of day,
Come take up your cin - ches, come shake out your reins,

The chuck wag - on's bus - y, the flap - jacks in play.
Come wake your old bron - co and break for the plains.

Move Along the Trail

Move to show the form of "Railroad Corral."

First and last Ⓐ sections:
Walk in time with the music, taking two steps per measure.

Second Ⓐ section:
Walk in a different direction.

Ⓑ section:
Stand in place and swing your arms.

Arts Connection

The Rattlesnake
by Frederic Remington
(1861–1909)

Remington's paintings and sculptures show action and motion. What action do you see in this sculpture? ▶

Sounds of the West

Listen to discover the form of this well-known American music. Try creating movement to show the form.

5-15
Cattle

**from *The Plow That Broke the Plains*
by Virgil Thomson**

This piece combines three cowboy waltz melodies.

Soaring Melodies

"Now Let Me Fly" is an African American spiritual. Many spirituals speak of flying away. During the time of slavery, to "fly away" often meant to escape to freedom.

Listen to the recording. **Sing** pitch syllables with the refrain. How many different pitches are there?

5-16

Now Let Me Fly

African American Spiritual

REFRAIN

Now let me fly, _____ Now let me fly, _____

Now let me fly _____ way up high, _____

Way in the mid - dle of the air.

Fine

174

Pentatonic Passage

Here are all of the pitches in "Now Let Me Fly."

so₁ la₁ do re mi so la

Since there are only five different pitches, this is a pentatonic song. What other pentatonic songs do you know?

VERSE

1. Way down yon - der in the mid - dle of the field,

See me work - in' at the char - iot wheel.

Not so par - tic - 'lar 'bout work - in' at the wheel,

D.C. al Fine

But I just wan - na see how the char - iot feels.

2. I got a mother in the Promised Land,
Ain't gonna stop 'til I shake her hand.
Not so partic'lar 'bout shakin' her hand,
But I just wanna get up to the Promised Land.

The Wind Blows Home

"Don't Let the Wind" is an African American folk song from an island off the Atlantic coast of the United States. The song starts on *mi*. **Listen** to the song. On what pitch does the song end?

5-18

Don't Let the Wind

Folk Song from St. Helena Island

do

Don't let the wind, don't let the wind, don't let the wind blow here no more.

Oh, _____ don't let the wind, don't let the wind blow here no more.

Sailing on a Melody

All of these pitches are in "Don't Let the Wind." Since the song ends on *do,* we say that *do* is the home tone. Read these notes.

do   re   mi   so   la   do'

Find these pitches in the song. Then **sing** the song with pitch syllables and hand signs.

Each of the melodies below is from a song you know. What is the home tone in each?

1.

2.

3.

St. Helena Island is off the coast of South Carolina. It is part of the United States.

A New Home Tone

"Erdö, erdö de magos" starts on *do*. **Listen** for notes in this song that are lower than *do*.

5-20

Erdö, erdö de magos
(In the Silent Forest)

English Words by Jean Sinor   *Folk Song from Hungary*

1. Erd - ö, erd - ö de ma - gos a te - te - je.
1. In the si - lent for - est sings the lone - ly bird,

Jaj, de ré - gen le - hul - lot a le - ve - le.
Cold winds blow - ing whis - per se - crets nev - er heard,

Jaj, de ré - gen le - hul - lot a le - ve - le.
High a - bove the moon re - flects an i - cy light,

Ár - va ma - dár pár - jat ke re si ben - ne.
Sha - dows flee - ing swift - ly through the au - tumn night.

2. Buza kozé szállt a dalos pacsirta,
   Mert odafenn a szemeit kisírta.
   Búzavirág, búzakalász árnyában
   Rágondolt a régi, els ö párjára.

2. Through the misty treetop flies the orphaned lark.
   Forest branches creaking stiffly, bare and stark.
   Sadly sounds the plaintive calling high above,
   Calling in the autumn shadows for his love.

Coming Home to *la*

This song has all of the pitches shown below. **Sing** them with pitch syllables.

la₁   do   re   mi   so   la

Now **sing** the song with pitch syllables as you point to each pitch.

Since *la* is the last pitch of the song, we say that *la* is the home tone.

The Night Will Never Stay

by Eleanor Farjeon

The night will never stay,
The night will still go by,
Though with a million stars
You pin it to the sky,
Though you bind it with the blowing wind
And buckle it with the moon,
The night will slip away
Like sorrow or a tune.

Flutes of the World

The flute is one of the oldest known instruments. Some type of flute is played in almost every country in the world. Sound is produced in different ways, depending on the type of flute.

Listen to these different flutes.

5-24
Flute Montage

▲ The Western **flute** is usually made of metal.

▲ **Panpipes** are single-tone flutes of different lengths bound together.

▲ The **shakuhachi** [SHAH-koo-HAH-chee] is a bamboo flute from Japan.

▲ The **sao** [dsow] is a bamboo flute from Vietnam.

Beauty in the Wind

Listen to this piece played by Jean-Pierre Rampal, who was one of the finest flutists in the world.

5-25
Sarabande

**from *Partita in A Minor*
by Johann Sebastian Bach**

Bach wrote music for flute and other solo instruments. He also wrote music for small ensembles and voices.

M·U·S·I·C M·A·K·E·R·S

Jean-Pierre Rampal

Jean-Pierre Rampal (1922–2000) was born in Marseilles, France. His father was a flutist and gave him flute lessons. During World War II, he was in his third year of medical school when the Nazis drafted him. He escaped to Paris instead and attended the National Conservatory. After the war, he became the first flutist in the Paris Opera Orchestra. Rampal won many awards and played with the world's major symphony orchestras. His wonderful musicianship will be remembered through the recordings he made.

Bring on the Brass!

If you've ever seen a marching band, then you've seen and heard brass instruments. All brass instruments have a mouthpiece, tubing that carries the air, and a bell that makes the sound louder.

Sound is produced when the player "buzzes," or vibrates the lips together while blowing.

Pressing the keys on some brass instruments opens and closes valves. This changes the pitch because the air travels through more or less tubing.

◀ Trombone

▲ Tuba

▲ Trumpet

Build Your Own Brass

To get an idea of how brass instruments work, you can make a simple one using a funnel, a garden hose, and a mouthpiece.

- Insert the funnel into one end of the hose.

- Put the mouthpiece into the other end.

- Roll up the hose to make it easier to handle.

- Buzz your lips into the mouthpiece to make sound.

Tune In

The tubing on brass instruments is all rolled up because otherwise they would be too large to hold. One type of tuba would be eighteen feet long if it were unrolled!

Video Library Watch *Arpeggio Meets the Brass Instruments* to learn more about them.

Tuba Talk

Listen to Deanna Swoboda discuss her career and her favorite instrument.

5-26

Interview with Deanna Swoboda

M·U·S·I·C M·A·K·E·R·S

Deanna Swoboda

Deanna Swoboda (born 1969) started taking clarinet lessons when she was in the fourth grade. In seventh grade, she decided to learn to play the trombone and then, the trumpet. Swoboda added tuba when she was in the eighth grade. Her father helped her carry the instrument to school and to rehearsals. She always wanted to be a professional brass player and teacher, and today she is.

Tuba Tune

Listen to this famous piece. It is usually not played on tuba.

5-27
Flight of the Bumblebee

by Nikolay Andreyevich Rimsky-Korsakov
as performed by Deanna Swoboda

This piece for solo instrument is originally from an opera.

The Brass Family

A brass quintet usually consists of 2 trumpets, French horn, trombone, and tuba. **Listen** to a part of Handel's *Water Music* played by Canadian Brass. What words would you use to describe the sound of these instruments?

5-29
Allegro Maestoso

from *Water Music*
by George Frideric Handel

Canadian Brass is one of the most famous brass quintets in the world. Each player is also a soloist on his instrument.

Canadian Brass

FUN WITH CANONS

Listen to learn the words of these silly rhymes. Then learn to perform them in **canon.**

Canon is a follow-the-leader process in which all perform the same pattern, but start at different times.

6-1

Table Manners

Anonymous

Rhythmic Setting by Konnie Saliba

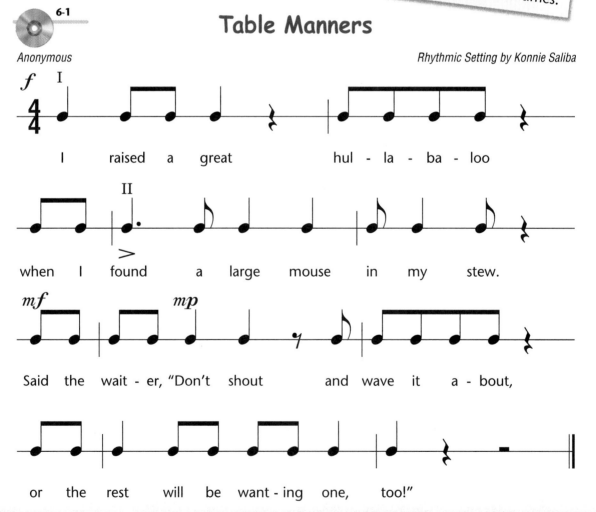

f I

I raised a great hul - la - ba - loo

II

when I found a large mouse in my stew.

mf *mp*

Said the wait - er, "Don't shout and wave it a - bout,

or the rest will be want - ing one, too!"

There Was an Old Man

Edward Lear

Rhythmic Setting by Konnie Saliba

I **mp**

There was an old man with a beard,

II

crescendo to end

who said, "It's just as I feared!

Two owls and a hen, four larks and a wren,

ff

have all built their nests in my beard!"

Speech Texture

Create a piece with many different layers of sound.

• Pat and clap this accompaniment as you speak this piece.

clap
pat

• Now play the accompaniment on low and high timpani.

• Speak the poem once all together, then in a two-part canon.

Play a Morning Song

Here's a song you could use in your classroom every day.
Listen to "Good Morning," and then **sing** it with your class.

Good Morning

Words and Music by Elizabeth Gilpatrick

Good morn - ing, good morn - ing, I'm glad you're here to - day.

We'll do our work and have some fun and then go on our way.

You can also **sing** this song in canon. When you sing in canon,
be sure to listen to your part so you don't get lost!

Play and Sing

Play this recorder part while your class **sings** the song.

Canon Call

You can perform "Good Morning" in many different ways.
Try it with and without accompaniment. **Sing** it in unison and
in canon. Which way has the thinnest texture? the thickest?

Singing Together

When singing in parts, you should always

• **Sing** your own part until you know it by heart.

• Practice listening to the second part while you **sing** your own.

• **Listen** to be sure your group is singing in tune.

Putting It

1. Name these pitches using pitch syllables.

do

2. Which of these patterns shows AABA form?

a. ● ■ ▲ ▲ **b.** ● ■ ● ● **c.** ● ● ■ ●

6-7

What Do You Hear? 5A

Review the Sound Bank recordings of the instruments listed below. You will then hear three examples of different wind instruments. Point to the name of the instrument you hear.

1. a. flute **b.** panpipes

2. a. shakuhachi **b.** flute

3. a. trumpet **b.** tuba

6-10

What Do You Hear? 5B

You will hear two musical examples. Pat a steady beat to discover the meter of each example.

1. a. $\frac{2}{4}$ **b.** $\frac{3}{4}$

2. a. $\frac{2}{4}$ **b.** $\frac{3}{4}$

All Together

Create a Canon

Create a speech canon. Work with a partner to write a four-line poem.

- Give lines 1 and 3 the same number of syllables.

- Give lines 2 and 4 the same number of syllables and make them rhyme.

- Decide where the second part of the canon should begin.

- Perform your speech canon for the class. Each of you can perform one part of the canon.

Music Is for Everybody!

How can you use the instruments named in this poem to **create** an accompaniment?

Music Class

by Kristine O'Connell George

I hear birds. I sing frogs.
My heart hears every note,
yet my song is locked
inside my throat.
Someone laughs.
I'm way off-key.

The teacher holds my hand
and opens a special box
of things with secret voices.

I get maracas and triangle.
I am aria. I am madrigal.
With silver bells and tambourine,
    I can sing!

Making Music our OWN

Sing a Lovely Song

There are many ways to make music your own. Singing, playing, and dancing are all things you can do to enjoy music. **Sing** this happy song with your classmates. Take turns singing the verses.

6-12

A Song of One

Words and Music by John Forster and Tom Chapin

1. Sing a song of one, one for the yel - low sun,

the yel-low sun that's shin - ing down on ev - 'ry - one.

2. Sing a song of two, two for the sky of blue, *(to Verse 2 ending)*
3. Sing a song of three, three for the red-wood tree, *(to Verse 3 ending)*
4. Sing a song of four, four for the sand - y shore, *(to Verse 4 ending)*
5. Sing a song of five, five for the things a - live, *(to Verse 5 ending)*

Verse 5 ending

G   D   *(to next line)*

a - live to leap   and soar ____ and dance a-long the shore,

Verse 4 ending

F♯   Bm   F♯   Bm *(to next line)*

the sand-y shore that joins the lea, the   lea where grows the   red-wood tree,

Verse 3 ending

A   D   A   D *(to next line)*

the red-wood tree that stretch-es high, high in - to   the   sky of blue,

Verse 2 ending

G   D   *(to next line)*

the sky   of   blue that shouts "Hal - loo," _____

Fine (after Verse 5)

D   G   D   G   D   A   D

to the yel-low   sun that's shin - ing down on   ev - 'ry - one.

Moving from

If music were always at one dynamic level, it might sound dull.

Composers include symbols in music that tell musicians when to make changes in the dynamic level.

A **crescendo** sign looks like this:

A **decrescendo** sign looks like this:

> A **crescendo** sign tells you to sing or play louder.

> A **decrescendo** sign tells you to sing or play softer.

Volume Control

Symphony conductors have many important jobs. They direct the players when to start and stop. They also help the players remember when to get loud and soft.

MUSIC MAKERS

JoAnn Falletta

JoAnn Falletta (born 1954) is an award-winning conductor. She received a doctorate from The Juilliard School in 1989. She has directed some of the great orchestras of the world, often being the first woman to do so. Falletta is known for conducting new American music. She has been the music director for the Buffalo Philharmonic, the Virginia Symphony, and the Long Beach Symphony orchestras.

Falletta is also known for her classical guitar playing, and has played with many great orchestras.

Loud

Dynamics in Action

Follow the dynamic markings as you speak this poem.

Singing-Time

by Rose Fyleman

I wake in the morning early

And always, the very first thing,

I poke out my head and I sit up in bed

And I sing and I sing and I sing.

Sound Waves

Listen to this piano piece, and raise your hand when you hear a *crescendo*. Where is the piece the loudest? Where is it the softest?

6-14
Valse Noble

from *Carnaval*
by Robert Schumann

This composition is one of many Schumann wrote for the piano.

Get on the Level

Find a space to sit on the floor. **Listen** to *Valse Noble*. Show the loudest part of the piece by spreading your arms as far apart as you can. Show the softest part by becoming as small as you can.

Listen one more time. Hold hands with a partner and show the dynamics by growing or shrinking in your space.

Robert Schumann

Robert Schumann (1810–1856) was twenty before he became a serious pianist and composer. He married his piano teacher's daughter, Clara, also a pianist. He wrote many types of music, including piano solos, pieces for ensembles, and songs. Some of his songs and piano pieces were written in sets. *Carnaval* is a set of 21 different piano pieces.

One of his piano sets, *Kinderszenen*, was written especially for children.

Tune In

Clara Schumann was a better-known pianist than her husband. Festivals are still held in Germany to honor her.

Web Site Go to *www.sbgmusic.com* to learn more about Robert and Clara Schumann.

Four Beats Together

"Turn the Glasses Over" is a song with meter in 4. This means that there are four beats in each measure, a strong beat followed by three weaker beats.

Create a four-beat movement with one strong beat and three weaker beats. **Sing** the song while you **move**.

6-15

Turn the Glasses Over

Folk Song from the United States

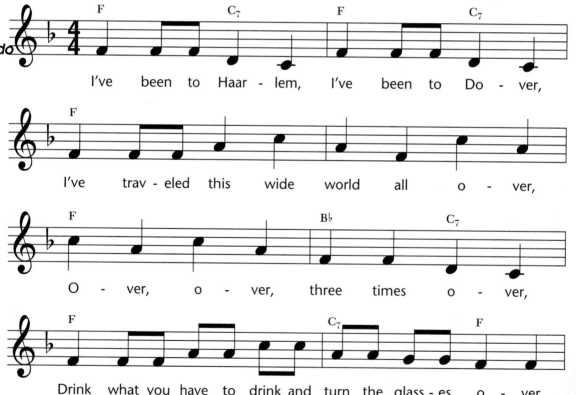

I've been to Haar - lem, I've been to Do - ver,

I've trav - eled this wide world all o - ver,

O - ver, o - ver, three times o - ver,

Drink what you have to drink and turn the glass - es o - ver.

A Game with Glasses

Play a game with cups or glasses to show meter in 4. Follow these directions.

1. Pick up your cup.
2. Turn it and tap it on the floor.
3. Pat the bottom of the cup.
4. Pass it to the left.

Sail - ing east, sail - ing west,

Sail - ing o - ver the o - cean,

Bet - ter watch out when the boat be - gins to rock,

Or you'll lose your girl in the o - cean.

UPBEAT OR DOWNBEAT?

In Israel, children plant trees on the holiday called *Tu b'Shvat.* This holiday is like a birthday party for trees.

Tap a steady beat as you **listen** to *"Hashkediya."*

6-17

Hashkediya

(Tu b'Shvat Is Here)

Words by M. Dushman

Music by M. Ravina

Hash - ke - di - ya po - ra - hat, V' she-mesh paz zo - ra - hat
The al-mond tree is grow - ing, A gold-en sun is glow - ing;

Tzi - po - rim me - rosh kol gag M' - vas - rot er bo he - hag;
Birds sing out in joy - ous glee From ev - ery roof and ev - ery tree.

Tu b' Shvat hi - gi - a Hag ha - i - la - not,
Tu b' Shvat is here, The fes - ti - val of trees.

Tu b' Shvat hi - gi - a Hag ha - i - la - not.
Hail the trees' New Year.____ Hap - py ho - li - day!

Pick Up the Beat

In what meter is *"Hashkediya"*? HINT: Look for the number of beats in a measure. Does the song start on an upbeat or **downbeat**?

Tap the beats in each measure as you **sing** the song.

> The **downbeat** is the beat that begins a measure.

Show What You Know!

Create a body percussion ostinato to perform with each rhythm below. Show upbeats and downbeats. How many beats are in each measure?

1. $\frac{2}{4}$

2. $\frac{3}{4}$

3. $\frac{4}{4}$

Tune In

Tu b'Shvat is a holiday for Israeli people to celebrate nature. They plant trees and eat seven foods grown in Israel: wheat, barley, figs, grapes, olives, dates, and pomegranates.

An Upbeat Lesson

"A Ram Sam Sam" is a song from Morocco. Moroccan music is usually very rhythmic, with lots of percussion. You might hear this music played with hand drums, bells, and cymbals. What rhythm instruments do you hear in the recording of the song?

Sing "A Ram Sam Sam" and pat the strong beats.

6-21

A Ram Sam Sam

Folk Song from Morocco

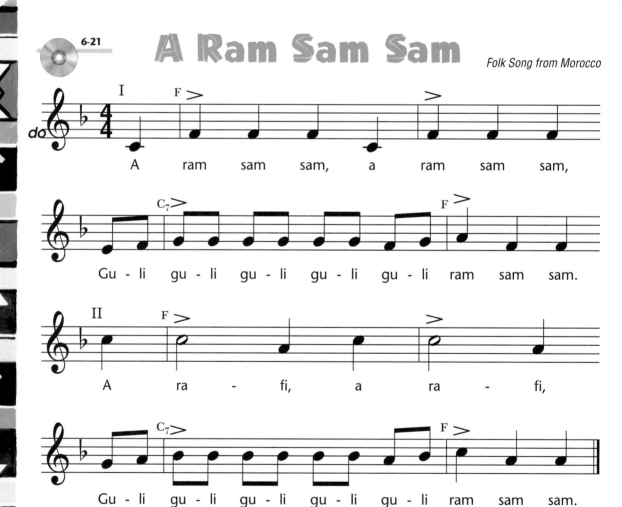

A ram sam sam, a ram sam sam,

Gu - li gu - li gu - li gu - li gu - li ram sam sam.

A ra - fi, a ra - fi,

Gu - li gu - li gu - li gu - li gu - li ram sam sam.

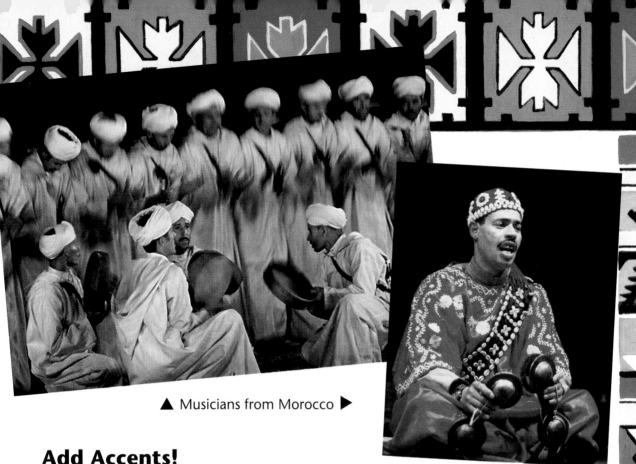

▲ Musicians from Morocco ▶

Add Accents!

Speak the words to "A Ram Sam Sam."
Say the upbeats softly. **Accent** the words that
occur on the strong beats.

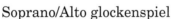

accent

An **accent** is used to give emphasis to a single note.

Parts to Play

Play this accompaniment to "A Ram Sam Sam."
Which part has accents marked on the strong beats?

Rondo-rama

This speech piece has three sections. Say the words to each section. Then **listen** to the recording to discover a new form.

6-23

Bananas and Cream

Words by David McCord

Rhythmic Setting by Konnie Saliba

A

Ba - na - nas and cream, ba - na - nas and cream.

All we could say was ba - na - nas and cream.

B

We could - n't say fruit, We would - n't say cow. We

did - n't say su - gar, We don't say it now.

C

We for - got it was fruit, We for - got the old cow. We

ne - ver said su - gar, We on - ly said WOW!

See a Rondo

Some music has several different sections. When is it performed, one section keeps repeating, while the other sections take turns. This is called **rondo** form.

A **rondo** is a musical form in which the **Ⓐ** section repeats between two or more different sections.

Which of these patterns shows the form you heard on the recording of "Bananas and Cream?"

1. Ⓐ ⬛B Ⓒ Ⓐ ⬛B

2. ⬛B Ⓒ Ⓐ Ⓐ ⬛B

3. Ⓐ ⬛B Ⓐ Ⓒ Ⓐ

Perform a Rondo

Here are some ways you can **perform** the sections of "Bananas and Cream."

- Speak the **Ⓐ** section.

- Clap the rhythm of the **B** section.

- Play the rhythm of the **Ⓒ** section on unpitched percussion instruments.

What other ways can you think of?

Move in Rondo

In what order would you **perform** these movements to create a movement rondo?

A

B

C

Create a Rondo

Now **create** a new movement rondo of your own. What three movements will you choose?

Hear a Rondo

Listen to this rondo for harpsichord and follow the listening map. How many different sections do you hear? How many times do you hear the **A** section?

6-25
Country Dance

by Charles Dibdin

This piece was written for harpsichord. A harpsichord resembles a piano, but its strings are plucked instead of hammered.

Country Dance

Listening Map

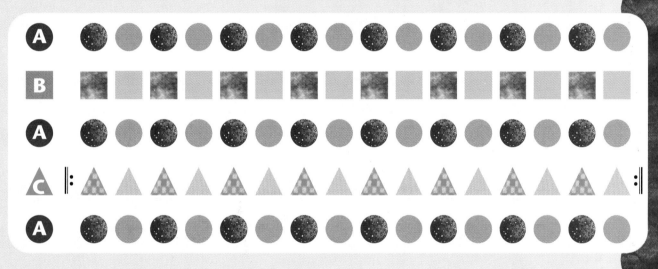

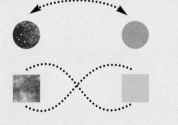

A   Tap knees with alternating hands.

B   Swish hands together.

C   Pat thighs using both hands.

Perform these movements as you listen to *Country Dance*.

A MICMAC MELODY

"*Kwa-nu-te*" is a gathering song of the Micmac of Nova Scotia, Canada. It is sung at the beginning of social events as the people gather.

Listen to "*Kwa-nu-te.*"

6-26

KWA-NU-TE

Native American Song of the Micmac

O kwa-nu - te ___ kwa-nu - te ___ kwa-nu - te ___ kwa-nu - tai

kwa-nu - te ___ kwa-nu - te ___ kwa-nu - te ___ kwa-nu - tai.

Kwa-nu - te ___ kwa-nu - te   Hey, kwa-nu - te ___ kwa-nu - te ___

kwa-nu - te ___ kwa-nu - tai.

What's the Tonal Center?

Look at the highlighted measure in *"Kwa-nu-te."*
This melody pattern occurs at the end of each phrase.
What is the last note of this pattern? When you find
the answer, you know the **tonal center** of this song.

The home tone of a song is also called the **tonal center.**

Play a Pattern

Pat this pattern as you **sing** *"Kwa-nu-te."*
Then sing the song again while you **play** the
pattern on drums.

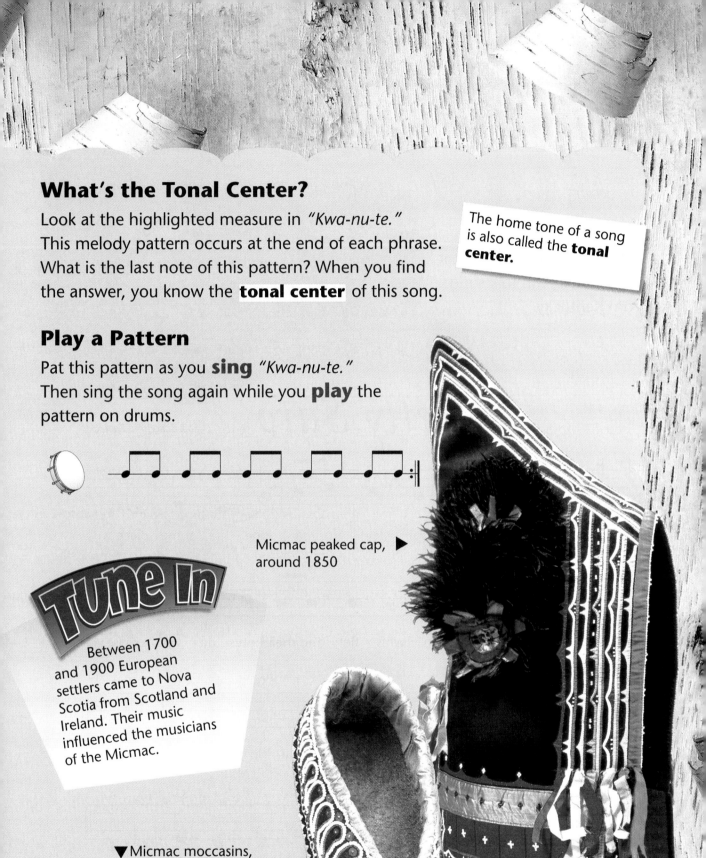

Micmac peaked cap, ▶
around 1850

Tune In

Between 1700
and 1900 European
settlers came to Nova
Scotia from Scotland and
Ireland. Their music
influenced the musicians
of the Micmac.

▼ Micmac moccasins,
around 1840

A New Tonal Center

Listen for the tonal center as you **sing** this folk song from Kentucky.

6-28

Pretty Saro

Folk Song from Kentucky

In some lone val - ley in a lone - some place,

Where the wild birds do whis - tle and their notes do in - crease,

Fare - well, pret - ty ___ Sa - ro, I bid you a - dieu,

But I'll dream of pret-ty Sa - ro where - ev - er I go.

Find the Tonal Center

Sing all of the pitches in "Pretty Saro," using pitch syllables and hand signs.

so,   *la,*   *do*   *re*   *mi*   *so*

You have sung songs that end on *do* and songs that end on *la.* On what pitch does "Pretty Saro" end? That pitch is the tonal center.

Show What You Know!

Sing each of these melodies with pitch syllables. What is the tonal center in each?

1. *do*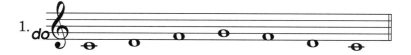

2. *do*

3. *do*

A Peddler's Song

Before supermarkets, people sometimes walked throughout the streets with carts to sell their goods. They would call out to get people's attention. "Hot Cross Buns" was a song a baker might have sung in England long ago.

Sing "Hot Cross Buns."

6-30

Hot Cross Buns
(Version 1)

Folk Song from England

Hot cross buns, Hot cross buns,

One a-pen-ny, two a-pen-ny, Hot cross buns.

Hot cross buns, Hot cross buns,

If you have no daugh-ters, feed them to your sons.

What's the Difference?

Here is the first line of the song written two different ways.
Sing these two lines with pitch syllables. Use the same syllables
for both. How are the two lines different?

1. mi re do   mi re do

2. mi re do   mi re do

Letter Names for Pitches

You have been singing melodies with pitch syllables–*do, re, mi, so,* and *la.* These syllables can be anywhere on the staff. Musicians can also use letter names for pitches. Letter names stay in the same place on the staff. This "musical alphabet" uses letters from A to G to name pitches.

This is the musical alphabet.

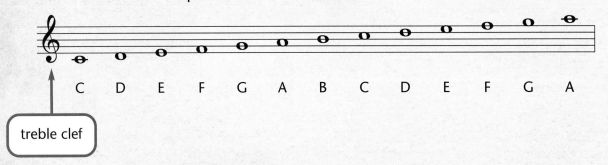

treble clef

The G clef, or treble clef, curls around the second line of the staff, which is home to the letter name "G."

A Recorder Song

"Hot Cross Buns" (Version 1) is a perfect song for playing on your recorder. **Sing** the song with letter names. Then **play** the melody on your recorder.

More of the Same—or Is It?

Clap and say the rhythm syllables of this version of "Hot Cross Buns." How is the rhythm different from the first version of the song? What else is different about the two songs?

Listen to this song, and then **sing** it.

Hot Cross Buns
(Version 2)

Folk Song from England

6-32

Hot cross buns! Hot cross buns!

One a pen - ny, two a pen - ny, Hot cross buns!

If you have no daugh - ters, Give them to your sons,

One a pen - ny, two a pen - ny, Hot cross buns!

Now **play** an accompaniment for this version of "Hot Cross Buns."

Recording Magic

Rick Bassett is a recording engineer. Each day he comes to work ready for new challenges.

Listen to Rick Bassett talk about his work.

6-34

**Interview with Rick Bassett
(Part 1)**

◀ Bassett records singers, instrumentalists, and narrators.

A recording engineer separates and then combines different tracks of a recording. Then he mixes all the parts.

An engineer can take samples of sounds from different places and change them to get exactly what is needed for a recording.

Words to Know

track—a single vocal or instrumental line that is recorded separately

mix—to combine different tracks for a final recording

reverb—a recording effect that creates the resonance, or sound, of different sizes and types of rooms

equalizing—changing the color of a sound, making it brighter or darker

mixing board—a master control board where all tracks are mixed and equalized before final recording

Working with Sound

In this part of the interview, Bassett discusses how he can change sounds that he has recorded.

6-35

Interview with Rick Bassett (Part 2)

More Than a Melody

"A Small Job" is a song with a simple melody. When you hear a melody, you hear only one pitch at a time.

Sing "A Small Job" and learn the melody.

6-36

A Small Job

Music by Jos Wuytack

Don't wor - ry   if   your   job   is   small and   your   re - wards are   few.

Re - mem - ber   that   the   might - y   oak   was   once   a   nut   like   you.

Tune In

The words of "A Small Job" are a proverb. A proverb is a wise, old saying.

Play While You Sing

Pat each of these patterns on your knees. Then **play** each of them on a mallet instrument.

Choose one of these patterns to add **harmony** to "A Small Job."

Another way to add harmony is to **sing** this song in canon. Look at the notation to find where to begin the second part.

> **Harmony** can occur when two or more different pitches sound at the same time.

Two-Chord Harmonies

"Vamos a la mar" is a song about a family who fishes for its supper. **Sing** "Vamos a la mar" and act out the words.

6-38

Vamos a la mar
(Let's Go to the Sea)

Folk Song from Guatemala

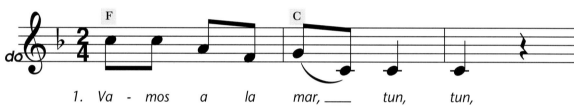

1. Va - mos   a   la   mar, ____ tun,   tun,
1. Let's   go   to   the   sea, ____ tun,   tun,

a   co - mer   pes - ca - do,   tun,   tun,
Hook   some   fish   and   fry   them,   tun,   tun,

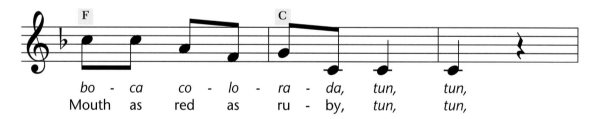

bo - ca   co - lo - ra - da,   tun,   tun,
Mouth   as   red   as   ru - by,   tun,   tun,

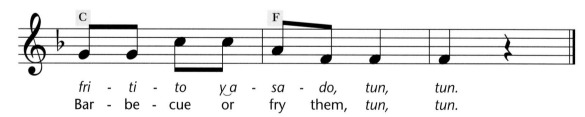

fri - ti - to   y a - sa - do,   tun,   tun.
Bar - be - cue   or   fry   them,   tun,   tun.

2. *Vamos a la mar, tun, tun,*
   a comer pescado, tun, tun,
   fritito y asado, tun, tun,
   en sartén de palo, tun, tun.

2. Let's go to the sea, *tun, tun,*
   Catch a fish and grill it, *tun, tun,*
   Barbecue or fry it, *tun, tun,*
   In a wooden skillet, *tun, tun.*

Sea Harmony

You can add harmony to this song by accompanying it with **chords.**

A **chord** is three or more different pitches sounding at the same time.

Use resonator bells to **play** the chords as your class sings the song. Follow the highlighted chord symbols in the song to know when to change chords.

▲ F chord

▲ C chord

Another Two-Chord Harmony

Here's another song that uses just two chords. **Listen** to "Sweet Potatoes" and find the chord markings in the music. Then **play** the chords on the Autoharp as you **sing** the song.

◀ Autoharp

6-42

Sweet Potatoes

Creole Folk Song

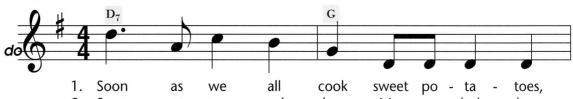

1. Soon as we all cook sweet po - ta - toes,
2. Soon as sup - per's done, Ma - ma hol - lers,

Sweet po - ta - toes, Sweet po - ta - toes,
Ma - ma hol - lers, Ma - ma hol - lers,

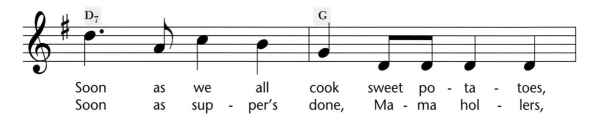

Soon as we all cook sweet po - ta - toes,
Soon as sup - per's done, Ma - ma hol - lers,

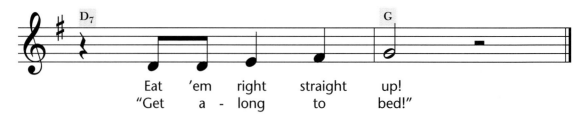

Eat 'em right straight up!
"Get a - long to bed!"

3. Soon's we touch our heads to the pillow, . . .
Go to sleep right smart!

4. Soon's the rooster crow in the mornin', . . .
Gotta wash our face!

Add a Layer

Play this bass metallophone part to add another layer of harmony to "Sweet Potatoes."

A Song in a Song

Listen to hear the "Sweet Potatoes" melody in this piano piece.

6-43
Bamboula

by Louis Moreau Gottschalk

Gottschalk wrote *Bamboula* when he was only twenty years old.

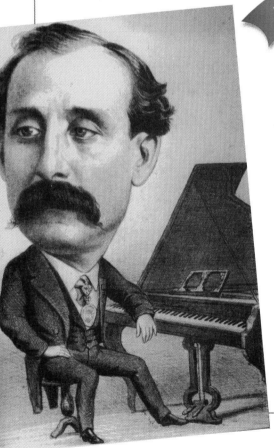

M·U·S·I·C M·A·K·E·R·S

Louis Moreau Gottschalk

Louis Moreau Gottschalk (1829–1869) was born in New Orleans. When he was only four years old, he could pick out tunes on the piano. At age thirteen, he went to study in Paris. He played his first recital there at sixteen. Gottschalk was one of the first American composers to incorporate folk songs into his music. He often used Creole folk melodies from Louisiana, where he grew up. He loved to travel throughout the world to play the piano and spread goodwill.

A World of Textures

Sing "He's Got the Whole World in His Hands," a very famous spiritual. What clapping pattern could you use as you **sing**?

6-44 **He's Got the Whole World in His Hands**

African American Spiritual

1. He's got the whole world _ in his hands, ___

He's got the whole world _ in his hands, ___

He's got the whole world _ in his hands, ___

He's got the whole world in his hands. _____

2. He's got the wind and rain in his hands, *(3 times)*
He's got the whole world in his hands.

3. He's got-a you and me, brother, in his hands,
He's got-a you and me, sister, in his hands,
He's got-a you and me, brother, in his hands,
He's got the whole world in his hands.

Adding Texture

Create an accompaniment to change the texture of "He's Got the Whole World in His Hands." Choose an unpitched percussion instrument and **play** a short rhythm pattern as the class sings verse 1. Then **play** a rain stick and wind chimes for verse 2. Add temple blocks for verse 3.

Move to the Music

Add these movements as you sing.

whole world

wind

you and me, brother

UNIT 6

Putting It

What Do You Know?

1. Add the correct number of quarter notes to complete each measure.

2. Read each set of letter names below. What words do they spell?

3. Match each vocabulary word to its definition.

a. *crescendo*   • gradually get softer

b. *decrescendo*   • two or more pitches sound at the same time

c. rondo   • gradually get louder

d. harmony   • Ⓐ section repeats between two or
                            more different sections

6-45

What Do You Hear? 6

You will hear three selections. Point to the sign that describes the dynamics you hear.

1.

2.

3.

228

All Together

What You Can Do

Play Chords

Look at the notation for "Sweet Potatoes" on page 224.

- Find the chords marked in the notation.
- Strum the chords on Autoharp as you sing.
- Create a one-measure rhythm pattern.
- Strum the chords, using your created rhythm, as the class sings the song.

Create a Rondo

You can create your own rondo.

- Create a four-line poem to use as an **A** section.
- Use body percussion, instruments, or movement to create a **B** and a **C** section.
- Perform your sections in rondo form.

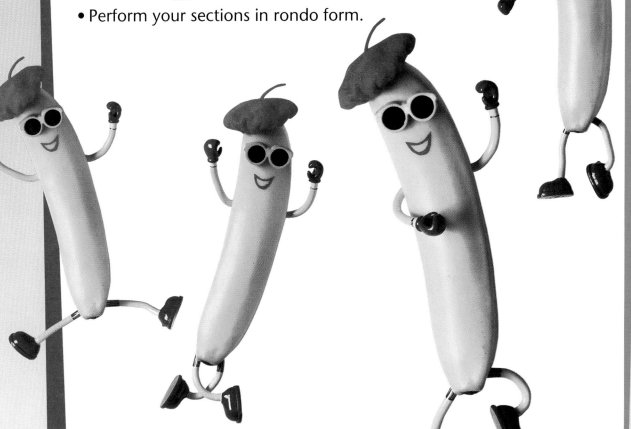

PATHS TO MAKING MUSIC

Can You Hear It?

Walt Whitman, an American poet, celebrated our country in a long poem called "I Hear America Singing." Here is part of his poem.

I Hear America Singing (excerpt)
by Walt Whitman

I hear America singing, the varied carols I hear. . .

Each singing what belongs to him or her and to none else.

Use Your Voice

Create your own poem about America.

• Make your poem at least four lines long.

• Practice reading your poem with feeling.

• Think about musical sounds you could use to accompany your poem.

• Create an accompaniment.

• Perform your poem with accompaniment.

Singing America

The United States is a country of many singers and many songs. What is your favorite American song?

Sing Across the Land

All across the United States, people enjoy singing together. Get ready to **sing** about the different people and places in our country.

6-48

Sing, America, Sing!

Words and Music by Jill Gallina

do

Sing, A - mer - i - ca, sing!   Lift up your voice __ in a song.

Sing, A - mer - i - ca, sing!   Sing with a voice __ proud and strong.

With man-y fac - es from man-y pla - ces, A   joy-ful mes-sage we bring,

A   cel - e - bra - tion a - cross our na - tion, Let mer - ry mu - sic ring!

Sing, A - mer - i - ca, sing!   Lift up your voice __ in a song.

Sing, A - mer - i - ca, sing!   Sing with a   voice—proud and strong.

With songs we greet—you, as   now we treat — you to a world of mel - o - dies.

So   lift up your voice — in a   song,   and   soon all A - mer - i - ca

2nd time to Coda   **8**   *D. S. al Coda*   **9**

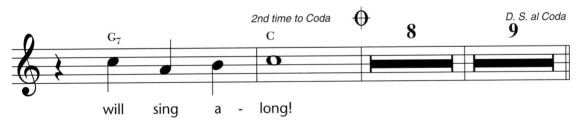

will   sing   a - long!

Sing, A - mer - i - ca, sing A - mer - i - ca, sing!

BUILDING WITH SONG

Have you ever helped to build a doghouse, a tree house, or a birdhouse?

"Bling Blang" is a song about the sounds of building. Woody Guthrie, an American folksinger, wrote it for his children. **Listen** to the song, and then **sing** along.

BLING BLANG

7-1

Words and Music by Woody Guthrie

VERSE

do

1. You get a ham-mer and I'll get a nail;

You catch a bird and I'll catch a snail;

You bring a board and I'll bring a saw, and

we'll build a house for the ba - by - o.

Bling blang, ham-mer with my ham-mer,

Zing - o zang - o, cut-ting with my saw.

2. I'll grab some mud and you grab some clay
   So when it rains it won't wash away.
   We'll build a house that'll be so strong,
   The winds will sing my baby a song. *Refrain*

Building America

Listen to this recording by the folk group The Weavers. What do the singers want to build in this song?

 7-3
If I Had a Hammer

by Pete Seeger

This is a song that was written and sung during the civil rights movement of the 1960s.

M·U·S·I·C M·A·K·E·R·S

THE WEAVERS

The Weavers are known as the first successful folk group in mainstream popular music. They first sang together in 1948. The members were Pete Seeger, Lee Hayes, Fred Hellerman, Ronnie Gilbert, Erik Darling, and Frank Hamilton. Nearly all of the Weavers' records became hits. One of their best-known songs was "Goodnight Irene." It sold one million copies in 1950.

For fifteen years the Weavers traveled widely and made many recordings. In 1963 the group performed a final concert at Carnegie Hall in New York.

Singing on the Railroad

Singing can make work more fun. Workers on the Transcontinental Railway in the 1860s sang songs as they built railroad tracks across the United States.

Sing along with this famous railroad song.

7-4

I've Been Working on the Railroad

Work Song from the United States

A *With a swing*

I've been work-ing on the rail - road, All the live-long day;

I've been work-ing on the rail - road, Just to pass the time a - way.

Don't you hear the whis-tle blow - ing? Rise up so ear-ly in the morn.

Don't you hear the cap-tain shout - ing: "Di - nah, blow your horn!"

B G
Di - nah, won't you blow,

C
Di - nah won't you blow,

D₇
Di - nah, won't you blow your horn? _____

1. G
horn?

2. G

C G
Some - one's in the kitch - en with Di - nah,

G
Some-one's in the kitch - en, I

D₇
know. _____

G
Some-one's in the kitch-en with Di - nah,

C D₇
Strum-min' on the old

G
ban - jo.

G
Fee, fie,

3
fid-dle-ee i o,

fee, fie,

3
fid-dle-ee i

D₇
o, _____

slight ritard

G
Fee, fie,

C

3
fid-dle-ee i o,

a tempo

D₇
Strum-min' on the old

G
ban - jo.

Track the Sounds

Look for the Ⓐ, **B**, and Ⓒ sections of the song. **Create** a rhythm ostinato for each section. **Perform** your train music.

Singing on the Sea

A sea shanty is a sailor's work song. One sailor sings the verses of the song. The other sailors join in on the refrain.

"Song of the Fishes" tells the story of a fisherman and some sea creatures. **Listen** to the verse and **sing** along with the refrain. Imagine what might happen if the fish took over the boat!

7-6

Song of the Fishes

Sea Shanty from the United States

1. Come all you bold fish-er-men, lis-ten to me,
2. First comes the blue-fish a wag-ging his tail,

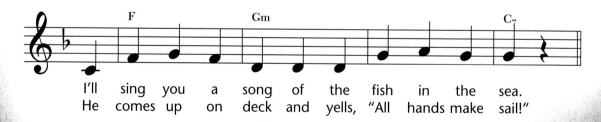

I'll sing you a song of the fish in the sea.
He comes up on deck and yells, "All hands make sail!"

Until I Saw the Sea

by Lilian Moore

Until I saw the sea
I did not know
that wind
could wrinkle water so.

I never knew
that sun
could splinter a whole sea
of blue.

Nor
did I know before,
a sea breathes in and out
upon a shore.

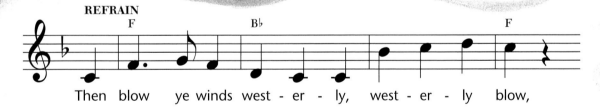

REFRAIN

Then blow ye winds west - er - ly, west - er - ly blow,

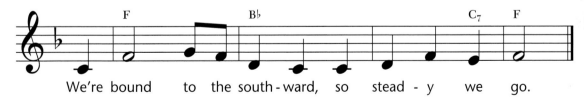

We're bound to the south - ward, so stead - y we go.

3. Next come the herrings
   with their little tails,
   They man sheets and halyards
   and set all the sails.

4. Next comes the porpoise,
   with his short snout,
   He jumps on the bridge
   and yells, "Ready, about!"

5. Then comes the mackerel,
   with his striped back,
   He flopped on the bridge
   and yelled, "Board the main tack!"

6. Up jumps the fisherman,
   stalwart and grim,
   And with his big net
   he scooped them all in.

Singing from the Heart

Music can help people express feelings. Spirituals are expressive folk songs, first sung by African Americans in the 1700s. **Listen** to "Peace Like a River." Think about the feelings expressed in this song as you **sing** along.

7-8

Peace Like a River

African American Spiritual

1. I've got peace like a riv-er, I've got peace like a riv-er,

I've got peace like a riv-er in my soul.

Signs of Peace

Learn to sign these words from "Peace Like a River." **Sing** the
song as you **perform** the signs.

peace   joy   love

I've got peace like a riv-er, I've got peace like a riv-er,

I've got peace like a riv-er in my soul.

2. I've got joy like a fountain, *(2 times)*
   I've got joy like a fountain in my soul.
   I've got joy like a fountain, *(2 times)*
   I've got joy like a fountain in my soul.

3. I've got love like the ocean, *(2 times)*
   I've got love like the ocean in my soul.
   I've got love like the ocean, *(2 times)*
   I've got love like the ocean in my soul.

Spiritual Styles

Listen to these spirituals as you look at the pictures of singers on these pages. What types of voices do you hear? Do you hear men or women? Do you hear children or adults?

7-10

Traveling Shoes

**Traditional African American
as performed by Sweet Honey in the Rock**

The women of Sweet Honey in the Rock have been singing together for more than 25 years. Their recordings include spirituals, children's songs, freedom songs, and movie soundtracks.

7-11

Ev'ry Time I Feel the Spirit

**Traditional African American
as performed by the Fisk Jubilee Singers**

The Fisk Jubilee Singers, from Fisk University in Nashville, Tennessee, has been in existence since 1871. They introduced spirituals to many people in their concert tours around the world.

7-12
He's Got the Whole World in His Hands

**Traditional African American
as performed by Marian Anderson**

Marian Anderson (1897–1993) sang all kinds of
music from spirituals to opera during her career.
Even though she faced discrimination, she
continued to sing and to break musical and
color barriers.

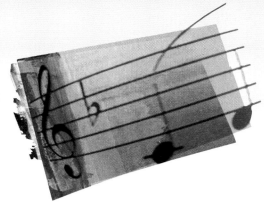

Tune In

"What is important
is if we are striving . . .
to do the very best that is
in us to do."
—*Marian Anderson*

7-13
Nobody Knows the Trouble I've Seen

**Traditional African American
as performed by the Boys' Choir of Harlem**

The Boys' Choir of Harlem was founded by Dr.
Walter J. Turnbull in 1968. The choir performs
spirituals, as well as other styles of music, including
jazz and classical. The Boys' Choir has sung all over
the world.

Singing for Fun!

Some songs are for working. Others are for having fun!
"Piñon, pirulín" is a song that accompanies a game played
in Central America. **Sing** the song and **listen** for clues
about how to play the game.

7-14

Piñon, pirulín

English Words by Ellen Traeger   *Folk Song from Central America*

1. Pi - ñon, pi - ñon, pi - ñon, pi-ru - lín, pi-ru-lín pi-ru - le - ro.
1. My friend, my friend, my friend, pi-ru - lín, pi-ru-lín, pi-ru - le - ro,

Pi - ñon, pi - ñon, pi - ñon, pi-ru - lín, pi-ru - lín, pi-ru - lón.
He plays u - pon the flute, pi-ru - lín, pi-ru - lín, pi-ru - lón.

2. Miguel, Miguel, Miguel,
   que la vuelta está a la derecha.
   Miguel, Miguel, Miguel,
   que la vuelta está al revés.

2. Miguel, Miguel, Miguel,
   To the right, to the right, pick a partner.
   Miguel, Miguel, Miguel,
   To the left, to the left, pick a friend.

The *jarana* [ha-RAH-nah]
is a guitar with eight
strings. ▼

Get with the Rhythm

Play these ostinatos to accompany *"Piñon, pirulín."* Tap and say the rhythm, then **play** the rhythm on the instrument shown.

Folk Style

Look at the folk instruments shown below. **Listen** for them in *El tilingo lingo.*

7-18

El tilingo lingo

Traditional Mexican

El tilingo lingo is a song about dancing. The words describe the sound of the instruments and the beauty of the dances.

The Mexican folk harp has more than 30 strings. ▼

▲ The *requinto* [reh-KEEN-toh] is a smaller guitar with only four strings.

Songs of CELEBRATION

All around the United States, people sing songs on special occasions. Singing helps people celebrate traditions and customs. What songs do you sing on special occasions?

Listen to "Inkpataya," a song sung by the Native American people of the Lakota nation. Sometimes this song is used for courting or for dancing at weddings.

7-19

Inkpataya

Native American Courting Song of the Lakota

Ink - pa - ta - ya   na - wa - zin   na - ya   si - na   ci - co - ze

ma - ya ___   ma - ya ___   le - ciya   ku   wa   na.

Listen to "Inkpataya" again. Tap with the beat as you listen. Does the tempo change or stay the same? Now **sing** the song.

Web Site Visit *www.sbgmusic.com* to learn more about Native American dance.

New Traditions

Listen to another version of *"Inkpataya."* This time the melody sounds like a lullaby. What instrument plays the melody?

7-24
Wioste Olowan Inkpa Ta-Ya

Traditional
as performed by R. Carlos Nakai

How is the melody played differently in this version?

M·U·S·I·C M·A·K·E·R·S

R. Carlos Nakai

R. Carlos Nakai (born 1946) is of Navajo and Ute heritage. He was born in Flagstaff, Arizona, and has played music of his people since his youth. Nakai has also studied the melodies of Plains and Woodlands people. He has developed his own style of playing the flute. It honors Native American tradition, but also includes new expressions. In 1992 Nakai became the second Native American to receive the Arizona Governor's Arts Award.

Songs of Honor

How many generations are alive in your family? Do you have grandparents or great-grandparents? Where do they live?

"O hal'lwe" is a song that honors the generations of women from the Nanticoke nation. The Nanticoke people lived in what is now Delaware.

Listen to *"O hal'lwe."* Tap lightly with the beat. Then **sing** the song.

7-25

O hal'lwe

Native American Women's Dance of the Nanticoke

Yu no he yu ne la, yu no he yu ne la,

yu no he yu ne la yu no he, yu ne la.

O hal' - lwe O hal' - lwe O hal' - lwe O hal' - lwe

O hal' - lwe O hal' - lwe he yo heh!

Powwow Dance

Listen to *Round Dance,* and think about what it would be like to take part in a powwow, a tribal gathering. **Move** your feet to match the tempo.

7-27
Round Dance

Traditional
as performed by Stoney Park Drum

This round dance is accompanied by vigorous singing and the steady beat of drums.

▼ Native American powwow

Birds of Fire

from the Passamoquoddy People

We are the stars which sing.
We sing with our light.
We are the birds of fire,
We fly across the heaven.

Arts of the Arctic Circle

The Inuit people live in the very north of Alaska and Canada near the Arctic Circle. They have developed styles of music and art that are unique.

Arts Connection

◀ Inuit artists are especially skilled at carving. This carving is made of soapstone.

MUSIC MAKERS

Tudjaat

Madeline Allakariallal and Phoebe Atagotaaluk are cousins and members of the Inuit singing group **Tudjaat.** Their music combines traditional song forms with popular music styles. The song *Qiugaviit* is an example of the combined style. Allakariallal and Atagotaaluk are also experts at throat singing. As they sing, throat singers imitate the sounds of nature, such as the calls of geese and whales.

An Inuit Song

Trace the shape of the melody of *Qiugaviit* as you follow the listening map below. **Listen** for the sounds of the wind at the beginning and end of the song.

7-28
Qiugaviit

Traditional Inuit (adapted)
as performed by Tudjaat

In this song, an elder is scolding a younger man for going on a hunting trip without dressing warmly.

Qiugaviit

Listening Map

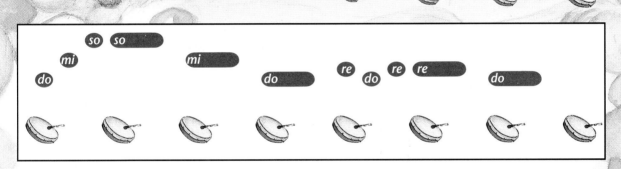

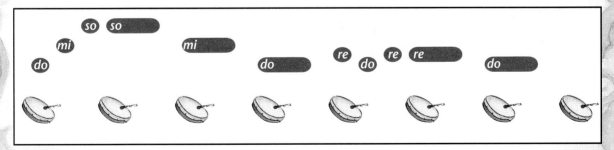

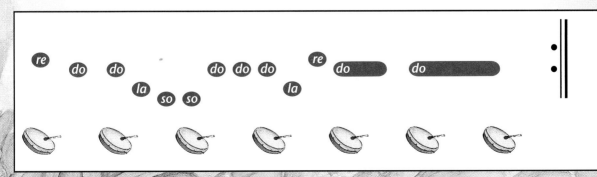

Songs of Nature

In Hawaii, nature is celebrated with songs, dances, and chants. **Sing** this song about the *hala* trees of Hawaii. As you sing, **move** to show the steady beat. Then use the chord symbols in the song and play an accompaniment on Autoharp.

7-29

Nani wale na hala
(Lovely Hala Trees)

English Words by Alice Firgau

Folk Song from Hawaii

Na - ni wa - le na___ ha - la,   E - a,   e - a.
Love - ly are the ha - la trees, ___   E - a,   e - a.

O   Na - u - e   i - ke   ka - i,   E - a,   e - a.
Sway - ing by   the gen - tle seas. ___   E - a,   e - a.

Ke ___   o - ni   a ___   e - la   E - a,   e - a.
Near Ha - e - na ha - las grow, ___   E - a,   e - a.

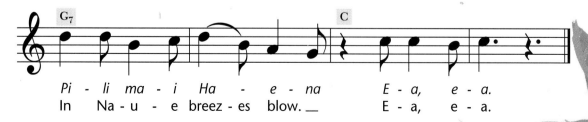

Pi - li ma - i Ha -   e - na   E - a,   e - a.
In   Na - u - e breez - es blow. ___   E - a,   e - a.

Playing *Puili* Sticks

Puili [poo-EE-lee] sticks are traditional Hawaiian instruments. They are made of bamboo. The bamboo is slit in many places, so it makes a rattling sound. You can **play** *puili* sticks in different ways. Try tapping them together, or against your hand. They are often played while dancing.

Move to *"Nani wale na hala"* while you **play** the *puili* sticks.

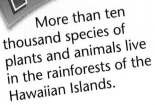

Tune In

More than ten thousand species of plants and animals live in the rainforests of the Hawaiian Islands.

Singing at the GAME

Have you ever been to a major league baseball game? If so, you probably sang "Take Me Out to the Ball Game" during the seventh-inning stretch. Stand up and **sing** this song.

Major League Melody

Look for the steps and skips in the melody of "Take Me Out to the Ball Game." Here are some clues.

1.

2.

3.

Tune In

The first official baseball game was played in Hoboken, New Jersey, in 1846.

256

Take Me Out to the Ball Game

Words by Jack Norworth

Music by Albert von Tilzer

Take me out to the ball game,

Take me out with the crowd.

Buy me some pea-nuts and crack - er - jack,

I don't care if I ev - er get back. Let me

root, root, root for the home team, If

they don't win it's a shame, For it's

one, two, three strikes you're out At the

old ball game.

SONGS FOR THE FLAG

Songs that express pride in our country are called patriotic songs. "You're a Grand Old Flag" is a famous patriotic song.

Sing the song and tap the steady beat. Then tap and say the rhythm of the first line. Which measure has a syncopated rhythm?

 7-36

YOU'RE A GRAND OLD FLAG

Words and Music by George M. Cohan

You're a grand old flag, you're a high-fly-ing flag;

And for-ev-er in peace may you wave;

You're the em-blem of the land I love,

The home of the free and the brave.

M·U·S·I·C M·A·K·E·R·S

George M. Cohan

George M. Cohan (1878–1942) was born in Rhode Island. As a boy, he performed in his family's vaudeville act. He became famous in 1904 as a character named Yankee Doodle Boy in the musical *Little Johnny Jones.* His song "The Yankee Doodle Boy" was first used in that musical. He wrote "Give My Regards to Broadway" and the World War I song "Over There." He also wrote about twenty plays and musicals.

Music Doodles

Listen for word clues that tell you this is a patriotic song.

 8-1

The Yankee Doodle Boy

by George M. Cohan

This song was used in several musicals other than *Little Johnny Jones.*

Ev - 'ry heart beats true un - der red, white, and blue,

Where there's nev – er a boast or brag;

But should auld ac - quaint - ance be for - got,

Keep your eye on the grand old flag.

The Small World of Music

All countries and people have special ways of using sounds to express themselves. Everyone has a special word for this— our word is *music.* You will hear many different kinds of music as you travel through this unit.

The different musical languages have their own ways of saying things. **Listen** to the bits of musical language on the recording. Can you match the music to the pictures?

8-2
World Music Montage

Our World of Music

What if you could travel outside your own country in song? In music, it IS a small world.

Many Languages, One Song

What do we mean when we call the world "small"? What makes it seem smaller today than it was fifty years ago? **Sing** along with this well-known song.

It's a Small World

Words and Music by Richard M. Sherman and Robert B. Sherman

8-3

VERSE

1. It's a world of laugh-ter, a world of tears,
2. There is just one moon and one gold-en sun,

It's a world of hopes and a world of fears.
And a smile means friend-ship to ev-'ry one.

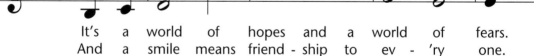

There's so much that we share, and it's time we're a-ware,
Though the moun-tains di-vide and the o-ceans are wide,

It's a small world af-ter all.

REFRAIN

It's a small world af - ter all,

It's a small world af - ter all,

It's a small world af - ter all,

It's a small, small world.

Let's Play with RHYTHM

"*Al tambor*" is a song about drumming. **Listen** for the rhythm patterns as you **sing** the song.

8-5

Al tambor
(The Drum Song)

English Words by Mary Shamrock

Children's Song from Panama

Al tam-bor, al tam-bor, al tam-bor de la a - le - grí - a,
Won't you play, won't you play, won't you play the *tam-bor - ci - to?*

Yo quie - ro que tú me lle - ves al tam-bor de la a - le - grí - a.
In time with the *tam-bor - ci - to* we en - joy our life to - geth - er.

Ma - rí - a, oh, Ma - rí - a, Ma - rí - a, a - mi - ga mí - a,
Ma - ri - a, oh, Ma - ri - a, this drum is a spe - cial trea-sure.

Yo quie - ro que tú me lle - ves al tam - bor de la a - le - grí - a.
In time with the *tam - bor - ci - to* we en - joy our life to - geth - er.

◀ The *caja* [KAH-hah] is a double-headed drum played with sticks.

The *repicador* [reh-PEEK-a-DOR] is a conga-type drum played with the hands. ▶

The *pujador* [poo-ha-DOR] is slightly larger and lower-sounding than the *repicador*. ▼

Drumming Is Fun!

Drums are important in Panama's traditional music. These three drums are often played together.

From your classroom instruments, select three different drums. **Play** the patterns below with the song. Play one part while your classmates play the others.

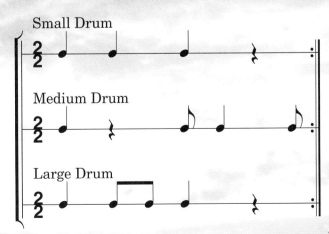

Small Drum

Medium Drum

Large Drum

A Song of Welcoming

Long ago people came to New Zealand from the Pacific Islands in large canoes. They called themselves *Maori* [MOW-ree], which means "people of the land." *"Karangatia ra"* is a Maori song of welcome.

Clap the strong beats as you **sing** the song.

Karangatia ra

Maori Action Song from New Zealand

Ka - ran - ga - ti - a ra __ Ka - ran - ga - ti - a ra __

Po - whi - ri - ti - a ra nga i - wi o te mo - tu

Ki te - nei ma - rae ha - e - re mai __

He hui a ro - ha mo kou - tou e te - i - wi

Na - u nei te a - ro - ha me te ma - mae.

Move to the Beat

This is a Maori action song.
Use these actions to **move**
to the music.

◀ *haere mai*

◀ *Karangatia ra*

me te ma-mae ▶

Arts Connection

◀ Maori wood carvings have different
styles depending on where the carvers
lived. Some carvings show wisdom.
Others show bravery. Some carvings
are meant to frighten evil away.

Arts of Cambodia

Classical dance is a treasured art form of Cambodia. It is the dance of the King's court. Children begin training before age 6 to develop the strength and flexibility needed to do this type of dance.

Listen to this classical music of Cambodia.

8-14

Mea haarit

Traditional from Cambodia

Mea haarit is an example of the classical music of the Cambodian royal courts. It is played during dance dramas.

Music of Cambodia

This popular Cambodian song is about the *sarika keo*.
This native bird can be tamed and taught to say words!

8-15

Sarika keo
(Bird Song)

English Words by David Eddleman

Folk Song from Cambodia

1. Sa - ri - ka keo euy   si ___ ey   kang ___ kang? Ey   sa - ri-yaing.
1. Oh, ___ ti - ny bird, tell me what   do   you eat? Ah   sa - ri-yang.

Sa - ri - ka keo euy   si ___ ey   kang ___ kang? Ey   sa - ri-yaing.
Oh, ___ ti - ny bird, tell me what   do   you eat? Ah   sa - ri-yang.

Si   phle   dam - bang   pra - choeuk ___ knea ___ leng.
A   cac - tus   fruit   so   ripe ___ and ___ sweet.

Euy   keo   keo ___ euy,   euy   keo   keo ___ euy. ___
Oy   koy   koy ___ oy,   oy   koy   koy ___ oy. ___

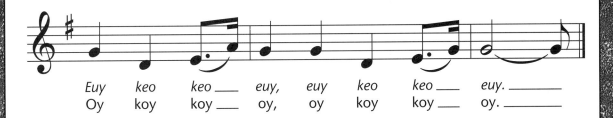

2. Slap vea chakk kbach
    moat vea thveu phleng.
    Ey sariyaing.
    (Repeat)
    Prachoeuk knea leng
    leu mek proeuksa.
    Euy keo keo euy,
    euy keo keo euy.

2. High in the sky
    you dance on the wing.
    Ah sariyang.
    (Repeat)
    High on a branch
    you fuss at everything!
    Oy koy koy oy,
    oy koy koy oy.

Frogs All Over

This counting song is well known all over the Szechuan [SEH-shwan] province of China. It is sung as a wish for peace.

Listen to hear how many phrases are in this song. Which ones are alike?

8-18

Shu ha mo
(Frogs)

English Words by Betty Warner Dietz and Thomas Choonbai Park

Folk Song from China

一 只 蛤 蟆 一 张 嘴
Yi zhi ha ma yi zhang zui
Each frog has a sin - gle mouth,

两 只 眼 睛 四 条 腿
liang zhi yan jing si tiao tui
He has two eyes and four legs.

乒 乓 乒 乓 跳 下 水 呀
Pin pong pin pong tiao xia shui ya
Ping pong, ping pong, count them with me.

Playing with Frogs

Here is an accompaniment to **play** while you sing
"Shu ha mo." Then create a frog dance you can
move to while you sing the song again.

蛤　蟆　不　吃　水
ha　ma　bu　chi　shui
Dur - ing　time　of　peace,

太　平　年
tai　ping ―― nian
frogs　do　not　drink.

荷　儿　梅　子　兮
he　er　mei　zi　xi
Wa - ter　lil - ies　float

水　上　漂
shui　shang　piao.
on　the　pond.

Sunshine and Song

This Russian song expresses the total joy of a perfect day—the sun is shining, the sky is blue, a child and mother are having a good time, and they hope it can last forever.

8-22

Pust' vsegda budet sonse
(May the Sun Shine Forever)

Russian Words by L. Oshanin
English Words by Alice Firgau

Music by A. Ostrovsky

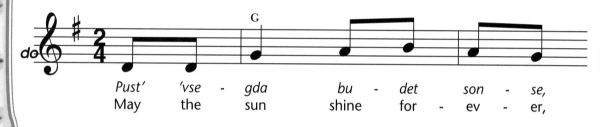

Pust'   'vse - gda   bu - det   son - se,
May   the   sun   shine   for - ev - er,

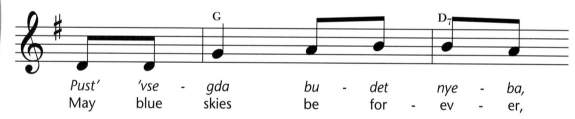

Pust'   'vse - gda   bu - det   nye - ba,
May   blue   skies   be   for - ev - er,

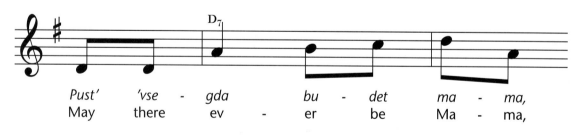

Pust'   'vse - gda   bu - det   ma - ma,
May   there   ev - er   be   Ma - ma,

Pust'   'vse - gda   bu - do   ya!   gda   bu - do   ya!
May   there   ev - er   be   me!   ev - er   be   me!

The Shape of Sunshine

Look at the four lines of the song. **Compare** the rhythm patterns. Which ones are alike?

Dancing for Joy

In northern Russia, winter can be long and dark. When the snow melts and the sun brings back blue skies, everyone celebrates. In the old days, children would play singing and dancing games in the countryside to welcome the spring.

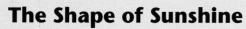

Follow the Form

Listen to this piece by a famous Russian composer. Follow the listening map to see the form.

8-27
Trepak

from *Nutcracker Suite for Orchestra*
by Piotr Ilyich Tchaikovsky

Trepak is one of a group of dances from the ballet *The Nutcracker*.

Trepak
Listening Map

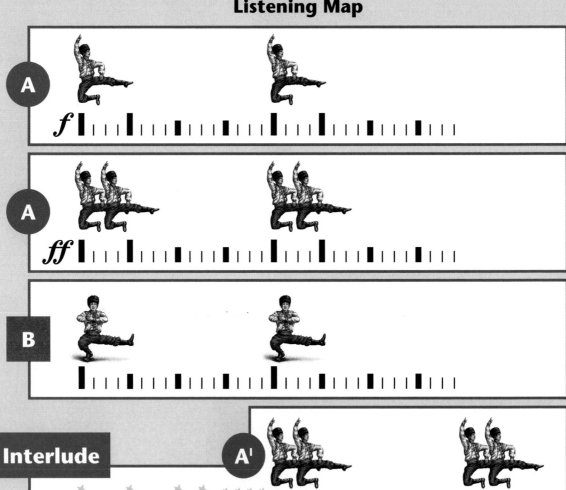

Piotr Ilyich Tchaikovsky

Piotr Ilyich Tchaikovsky [PYOH-ter IHL-yich chy-KOF-skee] was the first Russian composer whose music became well-known outside of Russia. His most famous works include *Symphony No. 5* and the ballets *Swan Lake* and *The Nutcracker.* He conducted his own music at the opening of Carnegie Hall in New York City in 1891.

Web Site Learn more about Tchaikovsky at *www.sbgmusic.com.*

Our World of Music

HAPPY BIRTHDAY!

"Mùbärak" is sung for birthdays in Iran. Guests are invited to the home. This song and the dance that goes with it are part of their celebration. Try to **sing** this at your next birthday!

This song has two parts, but you sing the first part twice. What is the form of this piece?

8-28

English Words by
Mary Shamrock

Mùbärak
(Happy Birthday)

Persian Birthday Song
As sung by Hooshang Bagheri

Mù - bä - rak,   mù - bä - rak,   ta - val - lu - det   mù - bä - rak,
Hap-py day,   hap-py day,   here it   is, your hap-py day.

mù - bä - rak,   mù - bä - rak   ta - val   lu - det   mù - bä - rak.
Hap-py day,   hap-py day,   here it   is, your hap-py day.

La bat shä - di de let khush,   chu gul pur khan-deh bä she
May this birth-day bring a   year   filled with all   the best for   you;

be - yä sham hä rä fot kun   ke sad säl zen-deh bä she.
As you blow the can-dles out,   may your spe - cial wish come true.

276

Everyone Loves a Birthday

Birthdays are special days all over the world. Look at these party pictures. What do they have in common?

◄ Germany

▲ Mexico

◄ Colombia

The Love of Country

This song expresses pride in the country of Israel. It speaks of joy in preparing the fields, planting the grain, and gathering the harvest.

Playing for Joy

Practice this ostinato. Then **play** it to accompany "*Artsa alinu.*"

Bass xylophone

Listen to find the steps, skips, and repeated pitches in the melody of *"Artsa alinu."* Then **sing** the song.

8-33

Artsa alínu
(Come to the Land)

Folk Song from Israel

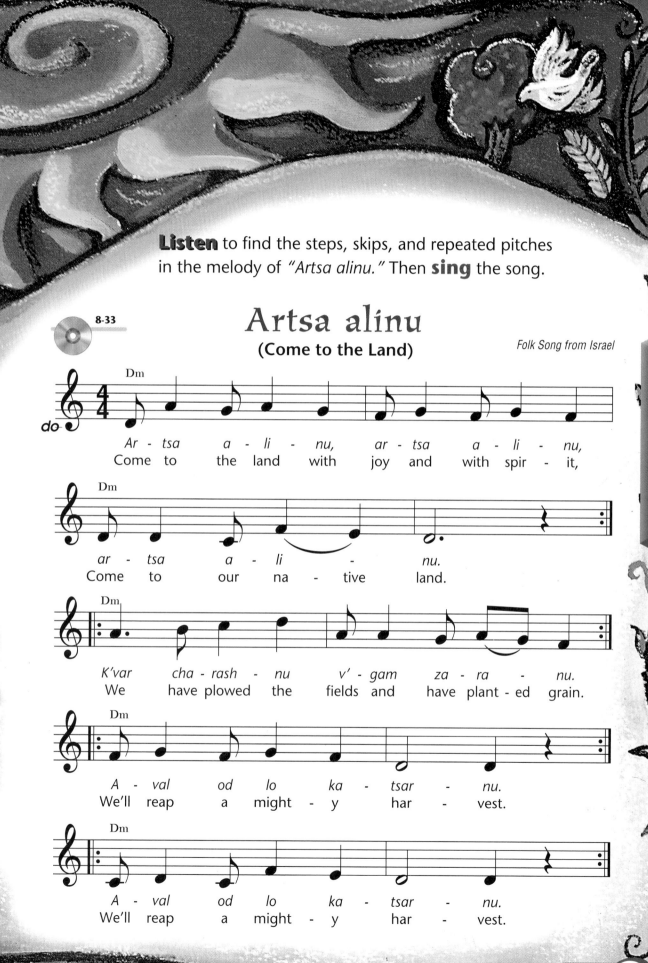

Dm

do

Ar - tsa a - li - nu, ar - tsa a - li - nu,
Come to the land with joy and with spir - it,

Dm

ar - tsa a - li - nu.
Come to our na - tive land.

Dm

K'var cha - rash - nu v' - gam za - ra - nu.
We have plowed the fields and have plant - ed grain.

Dm

A - val od lo ka - tsar - nu.
We'll reap a might - y har - vest.

Dm

A - val od lo ka - tsar - nu.
We'll reap a might - y har - vest.

Rhythms of Africa

"*Sansaw akroma*" is a song from Ghana that goes with a stone-passing game. **Listen** for the syncopations as you **sing** the song.

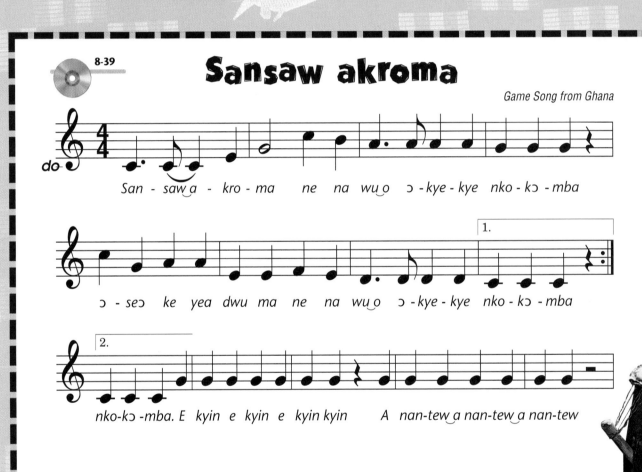

8-39

Sansaw akroma

Game Song from Ghana

San - saw a - kro - ma   ne   na wu o   ɔ - kye - kye   nko - kɔ - mba

ɔ - sea   ke   yea dwu   ma   ne   na wu o   ɔ - kye - kye   nko - kɔ - mba

nko-kɔ -mba. E kyin e kyin e kyin kyin   A nan-tew a nan-tew a nan-tew

Tune In

Ghana is a small country in West Africa. It has 72 languages, including an official sign language for the deaf.

Find the Form!

Listen to the song again. How many different sections do you hear? What is the form?

ɔ-seɔ ke yea dwu-ma   ne na ___ wu o ___   na je ___ wu o -   o

San - saw a - kro - ma   ne nay wu o   ɔ - kye - kye nko - kɔ - mba

ɔ - seɔ   ke   yea   dwu - ma   ne   na   wu o   ɔ - kye - kye   nko - kɔ - mba.

Drums from Ghana

Play a Rhythm Game

Play this game while you **sing** *"Sansaw akroma"* again.
Start with a small, smooth stone in front of you.

1. Pick up your stone and set it in front of the person on your right.

2. Pick up the stone in front of you and tap it once.

3. Set the stone in front of the person on your right.

4. Clap your hands.

Now, with your group, create your own stone-passing game. Try using two stones each. Share your ideas!

Listen to the Music

Listen to hear what instruments are included in this piece.

8-42
Awakening

by Osei Tutu

This song is part of a Ghanaian music tradition called Highlife. It mixes traditional drum music with jazz from the United States.

▲ Highlife musicians from Ghana

Sing of the Irish

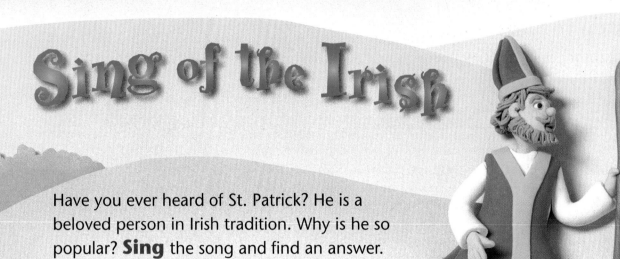

Have you ever heard of St. Patrick? He is a beloved person in Irish tradition. Why is he so popular? **Sing** the song and find an answer.

St. Patrick Was a Gentleman

9-1

Folk Song from Ireland

St. Pat-rick was a gen-tle-man, He came of de-cent peo-ple,

In Dub-lin town he built a church, And on it put a stee-ple.

His fa-ther was a Call-a-ghan, His moth-er was a Bra-dy,

Sounds of Ireland

Traditional Irish music is performed and loved throughout the world. The Irish harp has a very special timbre. **Listen** for it in the recording.

 ◀ Irish harp

His aunt was an O-'Shaugh-ness - y, And his un - cle was a Gra - dy.

REFRAIN

Then suc-cess to bold St. Pat-rick's fist, He was a saint so clev - er,

He gave the snakes and toads a twist, And ban-ished them for - ev - er.

The Sound of the Irish

Listen to this Irish song. The first instrument you hear is a pennywhistle. The pennywhistle is a traditional Irish wind instrument. **Describe** its timbre.

9-5 Roddy McCaulay

by The Clancy Brothers

The instruments in the accompaniment are added one by one–pennywhistle, guitar, and banjo.

M·U·S·I·C M·A·K·E·R·S

The Clancy Brothers

The Clancy Brothers moved to New York City from Ireland in the 1950s. They discovered a new way to perform traditional Irish songs that was appealing both to Irish Americans and to people who like folk music. They use guitar, banjo, pennywhistle, and energetic singing in their music.

Dance of the Irish

This is a dance similar to those you might see at an Irish dance party, or *ceilidh* [KAY-lee]. Try these dance steps with "St. Patrick Was a Gentleman."

The New-Found-Land

Newfoundland, a province in Canada, is well known for its fishing. This song is about a large port, called Bonavista, on the east side of the province. Fish are plentiful, so many people fish for a living. Clap to the beat as you **sing.**

Bonavist' Harbour

Folk Song from Newfoundland

1. Oh, there's lots of fish in Bon-a-vist' Har-bour,
2. Well, now, Un-cle George got up in the morn-ing,

Lots of fish right in a-round here. Boys and girls are
He got up in a won-der-ful tear. Ripped the seat right

fish-ing to-geth-er, For-ty-five miles from Car-bon-ear.
out of his britch-es; Now he's got ne'er pair to wear.

288

A Lively Work Dance

This song is definitely meant for dancing! It even gives you some of the directions in the song. **Move** to this song as you **sing**.

REFRAIN

Oh, catch a - hold this one, catch a - hold that one,

Swing a - round this one, swing a - round she. Dance a - round this one,

dance a - round that one, Did - dle dum this one, did - dle dum dee.

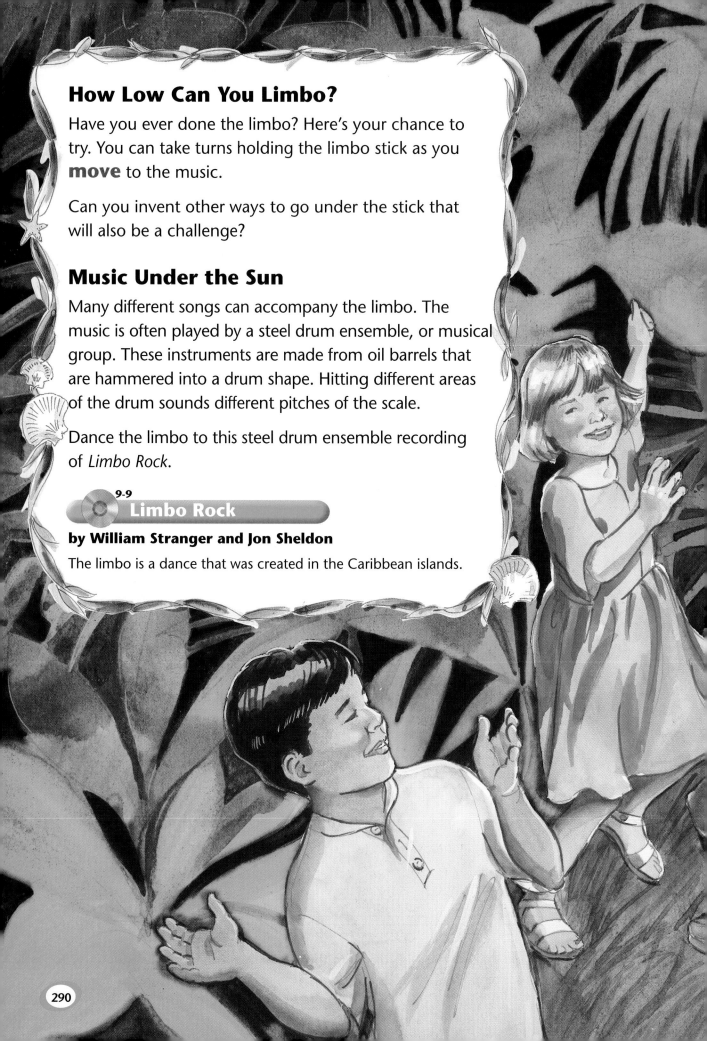

How Low Can You Limbo?

Have you ever done the limbo? Here's your chance to try. You can take turns holding the limbo stick as you **move** to the music.

Can you invent other ways to go under the stick that will also be a challenge?

Music Under the Sun

Many different songs can accompany the limbo. The music is often played by a steel drum ensemble, or musical group. These instruments are made from oil barrels that are hammered into a drum shape. Hitting different areas of the drum sounds different pitches of the scale.

Dance the limbo to this steel drum ensemble recording of *Limbo Rock*.

9-9
Limbo Rock

by William Stranger and Jon Sheldon

The limbo is a dance that was created in the Caribbean islands.

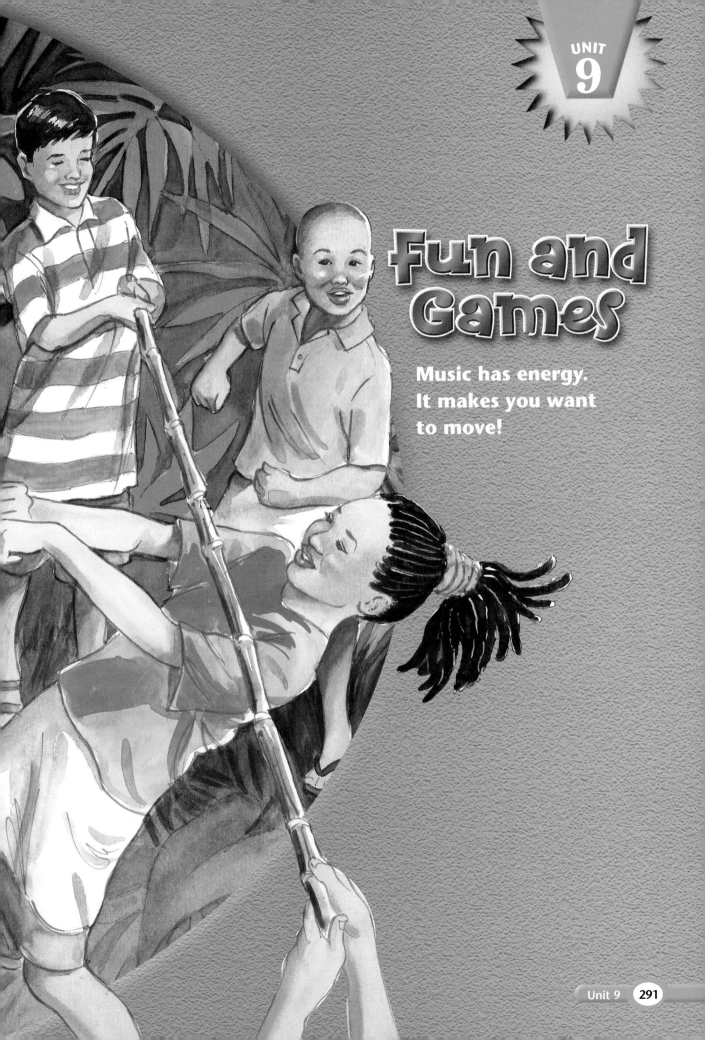

Fun and Games

Music has energy.
It makes you want
to move!

Sing, Dance, and Play

Music is used around the world for dancing and playing games. The songs in this unit will give you a chance to **move** in many different ways. Have a good time!

Children in Tobago like to sing this song while they clap in a circle. Learn to **sing** along with the song.

9-10

Poco, Le' Me 'Lone

Folk Song from Tobago

Po - co, le' ____ me 'lone, le' me 'lone,

Me no mar - ry yet le' me 'lone.

When me mar - ry, o bell go ring,

When me mar - ry, o shell go blow.

Po - co, le' ____ me 'lone, le' me 'lone,

Me no mar - ry yet, le' me 'lone.

Tune In

Caribbean weddings are sometimes celebrated by ringing bells and blowing conch [kahnk] shell horns.

Who Goes First?

"Jan ken pon" is a Japanese game for making choices. In the United States, the game is called "Rock, Paper, Scissors." People play it to decide who starts a game or who is first in line. **Sing** and play the hand game.

9-12

Jan ken pon

English Words by Mary Shamrock

Collected by Mary Shamrock at the Nishi Hongwanji Temple Dharma School

おなかがすいたらグーグーグー
O - na - ka ga su - i - ta - ra goo goo goo,
When you have a hair - cut, scis - sors snip, snip, snip.

かみのけのびたらチョキチョキチョキ
Ka - mi - no - ke no - bi ta - ra cho - ki cho - ki cho - ki,
Hun - gry sto - machs of - ten make a grum - ble, grum - ble, grum - ble.

ほこりをはたいてパーパーパー
Ho - ko - ri wo ha - ta - i - te pa pa pa,
Wip - ing with a dust rag makes a slap, slap, slap.

(Spoken)

ジャンケンポンでダーチョキパー　ジャンケンポン
Jan ken pon de goo cho - ki pa. Jan ken pon!
Snip, grumble, slap, now show me your hand! Jan ken pon!

choki

pa

goo

Make Your Own Sounds

Create an accompaniment to
"Jan ken pon."

• Choose three different small percussion
instruments for the words *goo, choki,* and *pa.*

• **Play** them when these words occur in the song.

• Use a wood block to play the steady beat.

• **Sing** the song as you play the accompaniment.

 Video Library See and hear how children from
other countries play singing games in *Singing Games.*

Catch a

Listen to the words of "Four White Horses." What do you think the *four white horses* might be? Why might a *shallow bay* of water be called a *ripe banana*?

9-16

Four White Horses

Folk Song from the Caribbean

Four white hors-es on the riv-er,

Hey, hey, hey, up to-mor-row,

Up to-mor-row is a rain-y day.

Calypso Beat!

Calypso Clapping Game

You can limbo to this song, or play a clapping game.

A Note Challenge

How many measures of this song can you find that have only one pitch in them? What is the letter name of this pitch? **Play** this note on your recorder.

Come on up ___ to the shal - low bay.

Shal - low bay ___ is a ripe ba - na - na,

Up to - mor - row is a rain - y day.

Play the Wichita Way!

Hand games are played by many native Americans. Game days are social occasions for people of all ages. Learn to **sing** these songs of the Wichita.

9-17

Wichita Hand Game Song 1

Game Song of the Wichita as sung by Stewart Owings

Hya ya ho we hya ya ho we hya ya ho we ya - o ya - o ho

9-19

Wichita Hand Game Song 2

Game Song of the Wichita as sung by Stewart Owings

Ya _____ we ha ya we ya _____ we ha

ya _____ we ha ya we ya _____ we ha ya we

Play the Game

Learn to play this game. Here's what you need.

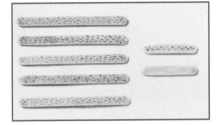

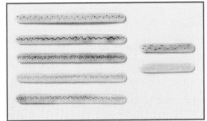

▲ counting and hiding sticks ▲ feather ▲ drum

Form two teams and sit facing each other. The "guesser" guesses in which hand the "hider" hides the short, marked stick. The team that guesses right five times wins!

Sounds of Brazil

"*Ah, eu entrei na roda*" is a game song from Brazil.
Listen to the song. How does the tempo change?

Sing the song before you learn the game.

9-21

Ah, eu entrei na roda
(I Came to Try This Game)

Circle Game from Brazil

Ah, eu en - trei na ro - da, pa - ra ver co - mo se dan - ça.
I came to try this game. __ I came to see the peo-ple danc-ing.

Ah, eu en - trei na con - tra dan - ça, Ah, eu nao sei dan - çar!
I came here to join the fun, but don't know how to dance!

La' vai uma, la' váo du - ás, la' váo três, pe - la ter - cei - ra,
There goes one and there goes two, there goes three, and on the third, There

la' se vai o meu a - mor de va - por p'ra ca - choi - e - ra!
goes my sweet-heart on a steam-boat down the riv - er to the sea.

Play an Accompaniment

Use resonator bells to **play** an accompaniment for *"Ah, eu entrei na roda."* **Play** these pitches on the steady beat.

Follow the chord symbols in the song notation to know when to change notes.

♫rts Connection

Tucanos com Bananeíras by João Batista Felga de Moraes ▼

Web Site Go to *www.sbgmusic.com* to learn more about Brazilian music and dance.

Come and Try This Dance!

Move as you sing *"Ah, eu entrei na roda."*

• Hold hands in a circle.

• Move into the center for four beats, and then out for four beats.

• Repeat the in and out steps.

• Skip to your left.

Now comes the most fun! **Play** the accompaniment, but go faster and faster as you play. The rest of the class can **sing** and **move** to the song. Try to keep up!

Hear the Brazilian Beat

Listen to this *Carnaval* music from Brazil.
Follow along with the listening map.

9-26

Um canto de afoxe para o bloco do ilé

by Caetano Veloso

Afoxe and *bloco* ensembles are usually made
up of cowbells, guitars, drums, and singers.

Um canto de afoxe para o bloco do ilé
Listening Map

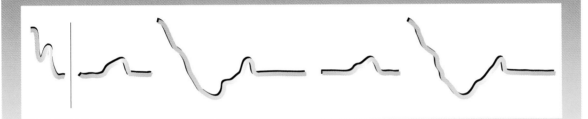

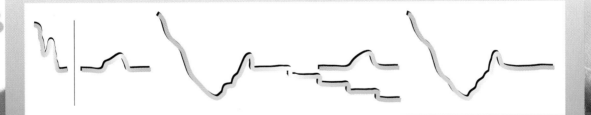

Lay It Down, Johnny Brown!

"Little Johnny Brown" is an African American game song. **Sing** the song and learn the motions.

Follow the Leader

Everyone enjoys being special. In this game you take turns being the leader. You can help each other by singing, clapping, and doing the motions with energy. Everyone gets a turn!

Tune In

The ring game is at least 100 years old. In this kind of game, the leader and group always take turns. This shows their support of one another.

Little Johnny Brown

African American Singing Game

Lit - tle   John - ny   Brown,   lay   your   com - fort   down,

Lit - tle   John - ny   Brown,   lay   your   com - fort   down.

Now   fold   one   cor - ner,   John - ny   Brown,___

Fold ___   the   oth - er   cor - ner,   John - ny   Brown.___

Call

Fold   the   oth - er   cor - ner,   John - ny   Brown,___
Give   it   to   an - oth - er,   John - ny   Brown,___
Make   a   lit - tle   mo - tion,   John - ny   Brown,___
Lope ___   like   a   buz - zard,   John - ny   Brown,___

Response   *Repeat 3 times*

Fold ___   the   oth - er   cor - ner,   John - ny   Brown._
Give ___   it   to   an - oth - er,   John - ny   Brown._
Make ___   a   lit - tle   mo - tion,   John - ny   Brown._
Lope _____   like   a   buz - zard,   John - ny   Brown._

'Round We Go!

This Polish folk song is written in meter in 3. Tap your foot on the strong beat of each measure as you **listen** to the song.

 9-29

Nie chcę cię znác

English Words by Mary Shamrock

(Don't Want to Know You)

Folk Song from Poland

Nie chcę cię, nie chcę cię, nie chcę cię znác.
Don't want to, don't want to, want to know you,

Chodź do mnie, chodź do mnie, rąez - kę mi daj.
Sor - ry, come back now, 'cause I real - ly do;

Pra - wą mi daj, le - wą mi daj.
Give me your right, give me your left,

306

Dance with a Friend

This dance is one of the first that Polish and Polish American children learn. The words of the song give cues for the dance steps.

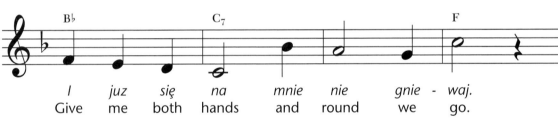

I juz się na mnie nie gnie - waj.
Give me both hands and round we go.

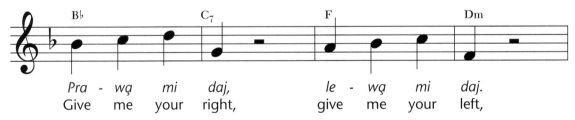

Pra - wą mi daj, le - wą mi daj.
Give me your right, give me your left,

I juz się na mnie nie gnie - waj.
Thank you, my friend, now off we go.

Saying and Playing Hello

When you visit a country, you need to learn a few expressions for greeting people and being polite. Here is a speech piece that will get you started for a trip to Poland.

Create a percussion accompaniment to this piece. Choose different instruments for the Polish and English words. Speak the words while you **play** the accompaniment.

Greetings

Words and Rhythmic Setting by Andrea Schafer

Cześć! Hel - lo! Dzień do - bry! Good mor - ning!

Bar - dzo mi - mi - ło. Pleased to meet you.

Dzię ku - ję. Thank you. Pro - szę. You're wel - come.

Prze - pra - szam. Ex - cuse me. Do - bra - noc. Good night.

Polish Rhythms

Listen to this famous *mazurka* by the Polish composer, Frédéric Chopin.

9-38

Mazurka, Opus 30, No. 3

by Frédéric Chopin

Traditionally, the *mazurka* is a Polish folk dance written in meter in 3. Chopin wrote 61 piano pieces based on this type of dance.

Tune In

The people of Warsaw, Poland, erected an enormous statue to honor Frédéric Chopin.

Fun and Games

Music in the Morning

"I Wonder Where Maria's Gone" is a song that was written to play at dances. Learn to sing this folk song from Kentucky.

 9-39

I WONDER WHERE MARIA'S GONE

Folk Song from Kentucky

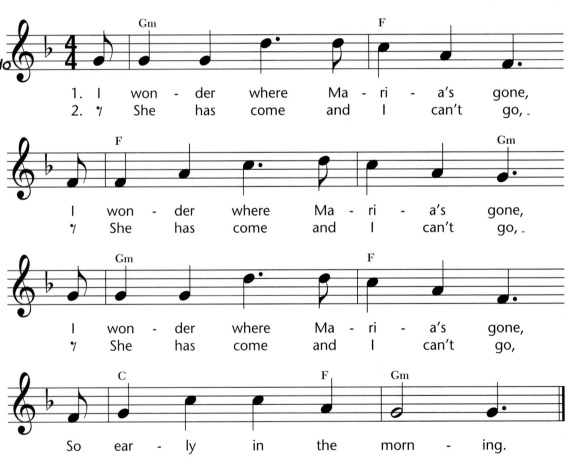

1. I won - der where Ma - ri - a's gone,
2. 𝄾 She has come and I can't go, _

I won - der where Ma - ri - a's gone,
𝄾 She has come and I can't go, _

I won - der where Ma - ri - a's gone,
𝄾 She has come and I can't go,

So ear - ly in the morn - ing.

3. Yonder she comes and "How do you do?"
   Yonder she comes and "How do you do?"
   Yonder she comes and "How do you do?"
   So early in the morning.

4. Shake her hand and wave on through,
   Shake her hand and wave on through,
   Shake her hand and wave on through,
   So early in the morning.

Dance in the Morning

Folk dancing is a very popular art form. You can **move** to a line dance while you **sing** "I Wonder Where Maria's Gone."

M·U·S·I·C M·A·K·E·R·S

GEORGE MARSHALL

George Marshall (born 1958) is a contradance caller and musician. A contradance is like a square dance, except it is done in lines instead of a square. First, Marshall teaches the dance steps with words. Then he plays concertina or *bodhran,* an Irish frame drum, with his band while the people dance. Sometimes he even calls the steps while he plays the music.

Marshall lives in Massachusetts, but he travels all over the country calling. He will work wherever there is a good wooden dance floor.

Fun and Games

Sing a Silly Song!

Sometimes songs have words that don't make any sense, but they are fun to sing. Here's an example in Spanish. A *citrón* is a lemon. *Fandango* and *rondella* are dances. Dancing lemons are very silly!

9-42

Al citrón

Latino Nonsense Song from California

Al ci-trón   de un   fan-dan-go, San-go, San-go, Sa-ba-ré.

Sa-ba-ré   de la   ron-de-lla Con su   tri-ki, tri-ki-trón.

Tune In

The *fandango* is a lively Spanish dance with meter in 3 that changes tempo.

I Was Walking in a Circle

by Jack Prelutsky

I was walking in a circle when I spied a piece of paper covered with a pretty picture colored yellow green and red as I picked it up I noticed that it also had some writing and I knew that I should read it this is what the writing said

Silly Games

Play a passing game while you **sing** *"Al citrón."*

The Earth Is Our Home

There may be many beautiful planets in the universe, but to us the most beautiful is our home, the Earth.

Speak with expression as you recite this poem.

Valentine for Earth

by Frances M. Frost

Oh, it will be fine
To rocket through space
And see the reverse
Of the moon's dark face,

To travel to Saturn
Or Venus or Mars,
Or maybe discover
Some uncharted stars.

But do they have anything
Better than we?
Do you think, for instance,
They have a blue sea

For sailing and swimming?
Do planets have hills
With raspberry thickets
Where a song sparrow fills

The summer with music?
And do they have snow
To silver the roads
Where the school buses go?

Oh, I'm all for rockets
And worlds cold or hot.
But I'm wild in love
With the planet we've got!

This Beautiful Planet

Composers often write music about the Earth and its beauty. What do you love most about planet Earth?

The Big, Blue Marble

Imagine what it's like to look at Earth from space.
Astronauts sometimes call Earth the "big blue marble."
Sing about our beautiful planet.

Big Beautiful Planet

Words and Music by Raffi

10-1

REFRAIN

There's a big beau-ti-ful plan-et in the sky, _____
And it's my home, _____ It's where I live.
You and man-y oth-ers live here too. _____
The earth is our home, _____ It's where we live.

Fine

VERSE

1. We can feel the pow - er of the noon - day sun,
2. We can feel the spir - it of a blow - ing wind,

A blaz - ing ball of fire ____ up a - bove;
A might - y source of pow - er in our lives.

Shin - ing light and warmth e - nough for ev - 'ry - one.
Of - fer - ing an - oth - er way to fill our needs,

A gift to ev - 'ry na - tion from a star.
Na - ture's gift to help us car - ry on.

Can You Cuckoo?

Many songs imitate the sounds of birds. **Listen** for the call of the cuckoo in this song. What instrument can you **play** to make the cuckoo sound?

10-3

El mes de abril
(The Month of April)

Folk Song from Spain

El mes de a - bril lle - gó,
The month of   A - pril's here,

y el cu - cu ya can - tó:
The cuck-oo's song we hear.

Cu - cú,   cu - cú,   el cu - cu ya can - tó.
Cuck - oo,   cuck - oo,   The cuck-oo's song we hear.

A Cuckoo Accompaniment

Play these accompaniments while you **sing** the song.

Glockenspiel

Alto Metallophone

Listen to this piece that was written almost three hundred years ago! Can you hear the call of the cuckoo?

10-7
Le cou cou

by Louis-Claude Daquin

Many composers have used bird calls as inspiration for their music.

Tune In

When a bird is born, it already knows how to sing part of the song of its bird family.

Let Your Spirit Soar

Plovers are birds that live near the ocean. Feel the long phrases as you **sing** the song.

10-8

Hama chi dori
(Plovers)

Words by Meishu Kashima

School Song from Japan
Music by Ryutaro Hirota

あ　お　い　つ　き　よ　の
Aa　o　ii　tsu　ki　yo　no
When　the　blue＿＿　moon　-　light

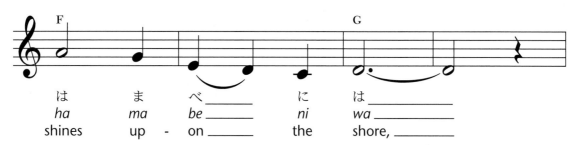

は　ま　べ＿＿　に　は＿＿＿
ha　ma　be＿＿　ni　wa＿＿＿
shines　up　-　on＿＿　the　shore,＿＿

お　や　を　さ　が　し　て
oh　ya　wo　sa　ga　shi　te
From　a　-　mong　the　gleam　-　ing　waves

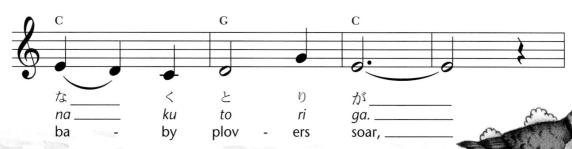

な＿＿　く　と　り　が＿＿＿
na＿＿　ku　to　ri　ga.＿＿＿
ba　-　by　plov　-　ers　soar,＿＿

Haiku for You

Haiku [hy-ᴋoo] is a three-line Japanese poem that is often about the seasons and nature. Haiku lets the reader imagine a scene.

Looking for the Mother Birds

by Issa, Haiku Master Poet

Warbler, wipe your feet neatly, if you please, but not on the plum petals!

な　　み　　の　　く　　に　　か　　ら
Na　mi　no　ku　ni　ka　ra
Look - ing　for　the　moth - er　birds,

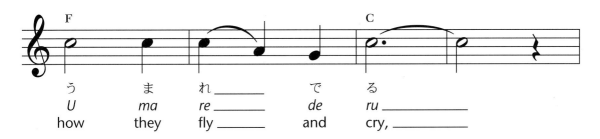

う　　ま　　れ＿＿＿　で　　る＿＿＿
U　ma　re＿＿＿　de　ru＿＿＿
how　they　fly＿＿＿　and　cry,＿＿＿

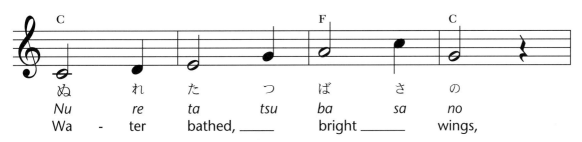

ぬ　　れ　　た　　つ　　ば　　さ　　の
Nu　re　ta　tsu　ba　sa　no
Wa - ter　bathed,＿＿　bright＿＿　wings,

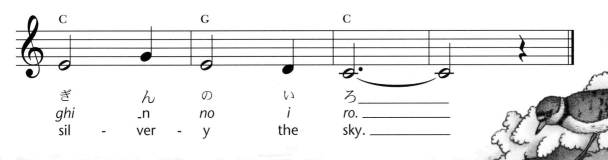

ぎ　　ん　　の　　い　　ろ＿＿＿
ghi　＿n　no　i　ro.＿＿＿
sil - ver - y　the　sky.＿＿＿

Music in Bloom

Gardens can grow most anywhere, in a backyard, on a windowsill, or on the roof of a building. What would you grow in your garden? **Listen** to "Garden Song."

10-12

Garden Song

Words and Music by David Mallett

1. Inch   by   inch,   row   by   row, ___
2. Pull - in'   weeds and   pick - in'   stones, ___

Gon - na make this   gar - den   grow, ___
Man   is   made of   dreams and   bones, ___

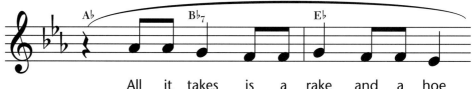

All   it   takes   is   a   rake   and   a   hoe
Feel   the   need   to ___ grow   my ___ own

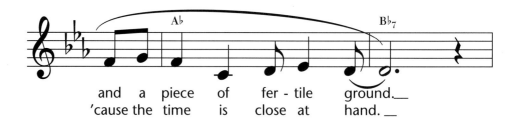

and   a   piece   of   fer - tile   ground. ___
'cause the   time   is   close   at   hand. ___

Garden Phrases

As you **sing** the song, follow the phrase marks in the music. **Move** in a new direction for each new phrase.

Inch   by   inch,   row   by   row, __
Grain   for   grain,   sun   and   rain, __

Some - one   bless   the   seeds   I   sow,
Find   my   way   in   na - ture's   chain,

Some-one   warm   them   from   be - low __
Tune   my   bod - y   and   my   brain _

'til   the   rain   comes   tum - bl - ing   down.
to   the   mu - sic   from _ the   land.

3. Plant your rows straight and strong,
   Temper them with prayer and song,
   Mother Earth will make you strong
   if you give her love and care.
   Old crow watching hungrily
   From his perch in yonder tree,
   In my garden I'm as free
   as that feathered thief up there.

Listen to the Rain

How hard do you think it is raining in this music? What "rainy" sounds do you hear? What instrument do you hear?

10-13
Jardins sous la pluie

by Claude Debussy
as performed by Arthur Rubinstein

The French composer Claude Debussy [DEH-bew-see] wrote this piece after visiting a friend's garden when it was raining.

MUSIC MAKERS
Arthur Rubinstein

Arthur Rubinstein (1887–1982) was a Polish-born American pianist. He came from a large family but was the only child who showed any musical ability. He developed a love of piano at an early age and gave his first recital at age seven. Rubinstein played all over the world. Several movies have been made about his life.

Gardens in Art

The French artist Claude Monet [moh-NAY] (1840–1926)
painted many pictures of gardens and flowers. Monet
designed his own garden at Giverny [zhih-vehr-NEE] in France.
He liked to paint the same flowers at different times of the day.

Arts Connection

▲ *Une allée du jardin de Monet*
(A Path in Monet's Garden)
by Claude Monet

This painting shows the many flowers Monet
planted in his garden at his home in Giverny.
He mixed simple and rare flowers together.

Tune In

"My eyes were finally
opened and I understood
nature; I learned at the
same time to love it."

Claude Monet

A Rabbit Tale

Storytelling is an important part of Native American tradition. **Listen** to this story of the Mohawk people.

10-14
The Rabbit Dance

Traditional Native American

Long ago, some hunters went out looking for game. When they got to an open field, what they saw amazed them. A giant rabbit, so big that it looked like a small bear, was standing alone. The hunters hid and watched. What they saw was remarkable. The large rabbit tapped a rhythm with its foot and, lo and behold, many rabbits appeared and started to dance.

Listen to the recording of *The Rabbit Dance* to find out why the rabbits were dancing.

Poetry Plus Percussion

Create a percussion accompaniment for "A Song of Greatness." **Play** your percussion parts as other students read the poem aloud.

A Song of Greatness

**from *My Song Is Beautiful*
A Chippewa Song**
Translated by Mary Austin

When I hear the old men
Telling of heroes,
Telling of great deeds
Of ancient days,
When I hear them telling,
Then I think within me
I too am one of these.

When I hear the people
Praising great ones,
Then I know that I too
Shall be esteemed,
I too when my time comes
Shall do mightily.

Canta, el sapito

Sometimes you can hear the sound of a small insect or animal but cannot see it. **Listen** to "*El sapito.*" Where do you think the toad is?

10-15

El sapito

(The Little Toad)

Words by Jose Sebastian Tallón
English Words courtesy of CP Language Institute

Music by Wilbur Alpírez Quesada

Na - die sa - be don - de vi - ve,   en la ca - sa no lo vió,
No one knows just where the toad lives.   We can't find him in the house.

pe - ro to - dos lo es - cu - cha - mos,   el sa - pi - to   glo, glo, glo.
But we know we all can hear it.   Lit - tle toad, sing glo, glo, glo.

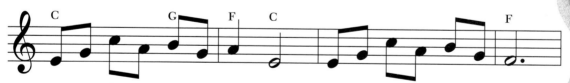

Vi - vi - rá en la chi - me - ne - a?   Vi - ve o - cul - to en u - na flor?
May - be liv - ing in the chim - ney,   May - be hid - den in a rose.

Don - de can - ta cuan - do llue - ve?   el sa - pi - to   glo.
When it rains where does the toad sing?   Lit - tle toad, sing glo.

"Toad-ally" Musical

Sing *"El sapito."* Which two lines of the melody are exactly alike? Which lines have the most skips in the melody?

Now **play** these ostinatos with the song. Then add another instrument to make a "toad sound."

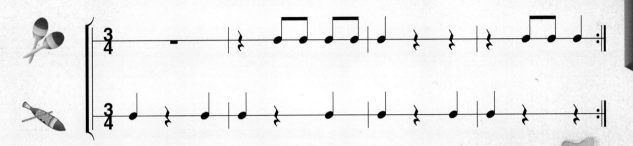

Our Mr. Toad

by David McCord

Our Mr. Toad
Has a nice abode
Under the first front step.
When it rains he's cool
In a secret pool
Where the water goes
     drip
     drop
     drop

Our Mr. Toad
Will avoid the road
He's a private-cellar man.
And it's not much fun
In the broiling sun
When you *have* a good
     ten
     tone
     tan.

Our Mr. Toad
Has a kind of code
That tells him the coast
     is clear.
Then away he'll hop
With a stop, stop, stop
When the dusk draws
     nigh
     no
     near.

Beautiful Day, Beautiful Song

Some days are so beautiful they make you feel like singing!
Make a list of all the beautiful things in this song. Then
sing the song in your most beautiful voice.

10-19

It's a Beautiful Day

Words and Music by Greg Scelsa

See the sun shin-ing in the win-dow, time to start a new _ day. _

Can't you hear the song-birds sing-in'? Got-ta sing out loud and say _

That it's a beau-ti-ful day _ for run-nin' in the sun, a
Yes, it's a

beau-ti-ful day _ that's just _ be-gun, _ a

beau-ti-ful day to do what I wan-na do, _ uh-huh! _

The Rhythm of Earth

What will happen to the Earth if we don't take care of it?

"Look Out for Mother Earth" is a song about our environment. It is in the style of a rap. Rap music began in the 1970s in New York City. The words are spoken over a rhythm accompaniment.

Write a Rap

Think of some words that have to do with saving our planet. Then use some of your words to **create** a rhythm pattern. **Play** the pattern on an instrument. Here are some examples.

1. Re - use   and   re - cy - cle

2. Save   the   Earth.

Speak Out for Mother Earth

Listen to the rhythms of the piece as you follow along with the words. **Sing** the refrain when you can.

 10-21

 Look Out for Mother Earth

Words and Music by Bryan Louiselle

VERSES

1. We gotta tell you, Mom,
    we gotta tell you, Dad,
   That we don't have
    ev'rything you had.
   We're not talkin' money
    or a life of ease;
   We're talkin' water, (Clean water!)
    clean water and trees.
   Hey, what's up with all the smoke
    from the factories?
   (to Refrain)

2. There's stuff goin' on
    that you can't even see:
   There's a hole in the sky
    where a hole shouldn't be.
   We're talking ozone. (Ozone?) Definitely.
   And if we don't cut back on C. F. C.s,
   We're gonna all need sunblock
    a thousand and three.
   (to Refrain)

3. Ev'ry fish and mammal,
    ev'ry insect and bird
   Makes a contribution,
    is a voice to be heard.
   Won't you hear the voice?
    Won't you feel the pain?
   They're sayin' oil spills!
    (Oil spills?) and acid rain.
   And everything else we're puttin'
    down the drain! Here we go again!
   (to Refrain)

4. Hey, teacher,
    won't you help us plot a strategy?
   Plan a plan for the planet.
    Plant a flower or tree.
   Promote ecological diversity.
   Not just for you, not just for me.
   It's for the kids
    in the next (Next!) century.
   (to Refrain)

REFRAIN

1. You got-ta look out, (Look out!) look out for the plan-et.

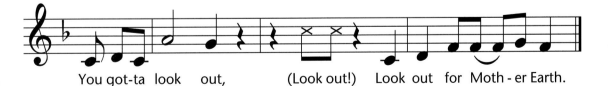

You got-ta look out, (Look out!) Look out for Moth - er Earth.

We Love the Earth

The world is full of beautiful places. Where is your favorite place? What do you see there? Think about this place as you **sing** "The World We Love."

10-23

The World We Love

Words and Music by Raffi and Michael Creber

REFRAIN

Here's to the world we love,

Blue skies and po - nies and child - ren at play,

Earth be - low, stars a - bove,

God bless it ev - 'ry - day.

Melody Moves

How does the melody of "The World We Love" move, by step or by skip? **Move** to follow the shape of the melody.

VERSE

1. Mist - cov - ered moun - tains that wel - come the sun,
2. Praise to the farm - er out work - in' the fields,

Buds on the branch - es, morn - ings be - gun,
Seed - ling to har - vest, food for our meals,

Dew - drops and blue - birds just start - ing to sing
Ma - mas and pa - pas, and hearts filled with love

D.C. al Fine

Praise for the brand new day.
For each and ev - 'ry day.

3. Here's to the rivers that run wild and free,
   The pull of the tides, the rush of the sea,
   Gold crimson sunsets to color our dreams
   In each and ev'ry day. *Refrain*

CELEBRATE NATURE!

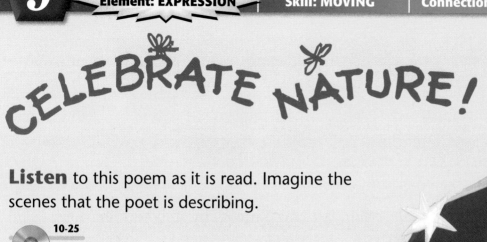

Listen to this poem as it is read. Imagine the scenes that the poet is describing.

10-25

The Song of the Night

by Leslie D. Perkins

I dance to the tune
of the stars and the moon.
I dance to the song of the night.

I dance to the strains
of a cricket's refrain.
I dance to the fireflies' light.

I dance to the breeze
and the whispering trees.
I dance to the meteor's flight.

I dance to the beat
of the summertime heat.
I dance to the pulse of the night.

Choices for Expression

Decide how you would like to read this poem. Think about different ways you can express the meaning of the words. Here are some suggestions to try.

• Vary the dynamics of each verse.

• Change the tempo of each verse.

• Choose some of the words and lines to repeat.

• Say the first lines of each verse one after the other.

• Experiment with saying the repeated words. Try using accents and different tempos and dynamic levels.

Create a Sound Symphony

Create sound effects to accompany your reading of "The Song of the Night."

• What instrument can you use to create a song of the night?

• What images or words can you express through sound effects?

• Look for other objects in your classroom you could use to create sound effects.

Create a Movement Symphony

Can the moon dance? Can stars, crickets, or trees dance? If they do, what does it look like? Try to **move** like this yourself!

Conduct a Symphony

Work with a group of classmates to create your own special performance of the poem.

• Choose one person to be the conductor.

• The conductor should give cues while you speak, play, and dance your symphony.

• Watch the conductor to know when to begin and to stop!

Story Time!

Stories and tales can serve many purposes. Some tell of events that happened many years ago. Others end with a moral. Some are told just to make us laugh!

Songs are often stories that are set to music. Sometimes it is easier to remember a story that you can sing. What songs do you know that tell a story?

Tell a Story

Make up a short story with two classmates. One of you can say the story, one can create movements, and one can play an ostinato. Together you can also create scenery by illustrating the story.
Perform the story for the class.

Tuneful Tales

Sometimes a song
can help to tell a story,
and sometimes the
song IS the story.

Tunes to Tell

"Sing Your Story" tells us different ways we can share stories and tales. **Sing** along with the recording.

Sing Your Story

Words and Music by Bryan Louiselle

VERSE

1. All a - round the world, in ev - 'ry time and place,
2. Fa - bles to ___ in - spire, or fair - y tales for fun,

Stor - ies help us learn a - bout the hu - man race.
Par - a - bles that teach a tale for ev - 'ry - one,

Leg - ends that we share, ad - ven - tures we ___ en - joy,
Stor - ies from the past and ev - 'ry dis - tant land

Bring us to - geth - er, ev - 'ry girl and ___ boy,
Bring us to - geth - er, help us un - der - stand,

Bring us to - geth - er, ev - 'ry girl and ___ boy. (So, come a - long now!)
Bring us to - geth - er, help us un - der - stand. (So, ev - 'ry - bod - y!)

342

REFRAIN

Sing your sto - ry! __ Come on, tell __ your tale! __

Make it up __ or just re-call __ what - ev - er hap - pened, big or small.

Oh, sing your sto - ry, ___ or write it for a friend. _

The best part __ is wait - ing at ___ the end.

SING DON GATO'S TALE

You know that there are different kinds of songs, like spirituals, dance songs, and echo songs. *"Don Gato"* is a **ballad**. **Listen** for the surprise ending!

A **ballad** is a song that tells a story.

11-1

Don Gato

English Words by Margaret Marks

Folk Song from Mexico

1. El se - ñor   Don Ga - to_es - ta   -   ba
1. Oh, Se - ñor   Don Ga   -   to was   a   cat,

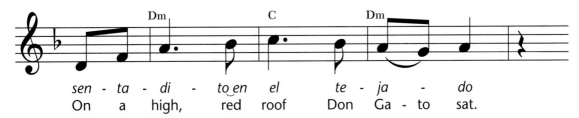

sen - ta - di - to_en el   te - ja   -   do
On   a   high,   red roof Don Ga - to sat.

cuan - do   le   vi - nie - ron   car - tas, mia - rra - miau,
He   went there to   read   a   let - ter, meow, meow, meow,

cuan - do   le   vi - nie - ron   car - tas, mia - rra - miau,
Where the read - ing light was bet - ter, meow, meow, meow,

si   que - rí   -   a   ser   ca - sa - do. ____
'Twas a   love note for   Don Ga - to! ____

The Pattern in Rhythm

Look at the rhythm of each phrase of the song.
Which phrases have the same rhythm?

2. *Con una gatita blanca,*
sobrina de un gato pardo,
que no la había más linda, . . .
que no la había más linda, . . .
en las casas de aquel barrio.

3. *Don Gato con la alegría,*
se ha caído del tejado;
ha roto siete costillas, . . .
ha roto siete costillas, . . .
las dos orejas y el rabo.

4. *A visitarlo venían,*
médicos y cirujanos;
todos dicen que se muere, . . .
todos dicen que se muere, . . .
que Don Gato está muy malo.

5. *El gatito ya se ha muerto,*
ya se ha muerto el buen Don Gato;
a enterrar ya se lo llevan, . . .
a enterrar ya se lo llevan, . . .
todos los gatos llorando.

6. *Cuando pasaba el entierro,*
por la plaza del pescado,
al olor de las sardinas, . . .
al olor de las sardinas, . . .
Don Gato ha resucitado.

2. "I adore you!" wrote the lady cat,
Who was fluffy, white, and nice and fat.
There was not a sweeter kitty, . . .
In the country or the city, . . .
And she said she'd wed Don Gato!

3. Oh, Don Gato jumped so happily,
He fell off the roof and broke his knee,
Broke his ribs and all his whiskers, . . .
And his little solar plexus, . . .
"¡Ay caramba!" cried Don Gato!

4. Then the doctors all came on the run
Just to see if something could be done,
And they held a consultation, . . .
About how to save their patient, . . .
How to save Señor Don Gato!

5. But in spite of ev'rything they tried,
Poor Señor Don Gato up and died,
Oh, it wasn't very merry, . . .
Going to the cemetery, . . .
For the ending of Don Gato!

6. When the funeral passed the market square,
Such a smell of fish was in the air,
Though his burial was slated, . . .
He became re-animated! . . .
He came back to life, Don Gato!

Listen to an Animal Beat

This song is about animals that might worry you. What did the composer do to add suspense to the song?

 11-5

If a Tiger Calls

Words and Music by Elizabeth Gilpatrick

1. If a ti - ger calls in the mid - dle of the night
2. If a li - on calls in the mid - dle of the day
3. If a croco - dile calls and in - vites you out to dine,

and in - vites you out for a lit - tle ev' - ning bite,
and in - vites you out for an af - ter - noon buf - fet,
tell him, "Thank you, ____ next De - cem - ber would be fine."

Last verse to Coda

do be war - y, for zo - ol - o - gists have shown that the
do be war - y, for zo - ol - o - gists have shown that the
And be war - y, for zo - ol - o - gists will state that the

ti - ger lies on the phone.
li - on lies on the phone.

346

croc - o - dile lies, the croc - o - dile lies,

the croc - o - dile lies in wait!

Play Body Percussion

• Speak the words of the song.

• Snap your fingers twice for the word *tiger.*

• Clap your hands twice for the word *lion.*

• Pat your knees three times for the word *crocodile.*

• Brush your hands together for the words *in wait.*

• Be sure you use a quiet, "sinister-sounding" voice!

The Panther
(excerpt)

by Ogden Nash

If called by a panther,

Don't anther!

Playing with Tigers!

Play this accompaniment with the first four lines of "If a Tiger Calls." **Create** a new verse about another animal.

Arts Connection

▲ *Surprised!* by Henri Rousseau [aw(n)-REE roo-soh] (1844–1910)

This painting is one of several famous jungle scenes by Rousseau. What do you think surprised the tiger?

Beastly Music

The lion is a very stately animal. It has padded feet and walks softly. **Listen** to *The Royal March of the Lion.* What instrument plays the lion's melody?

11-7
The Royal March of the Lion

**from *Carnival of the Animals*
by Camille Saint-Saëns**

Carnival of the Animals uses orchestral instruments to create images of animals through sound.

MUSIC MAKERS
Camille Saint-Saëns

Camille Saint-Saëns [kah-MEEL sa(n) SAW(n)] (1835–1921) was born in Paris, France. He composed his first piano piece when he was three years old. An excellent pianist and organist, he performed in many countries. He also composed music for piano, orchestra, and voice. *Carnival of the Animals* was a piece he wrote just for fun. Now it is one of his most famous compositions.

Tiny Boat Notes

This folk song from Latin America tells a story about a boat so tiny that it could not even sail.

11-8

El barquito
(The Tiny Boat)

English Words by Kim Williams   *Folk Song from Latin America*

Ha - bía u - na   vez   un   bar - co   chi - qui - ti - co,
Oh, there was once   a   boat so   ve - ry   ti - ny,

Ha - bía u - na   vez   un   bar - co   chi - qui - ti - co,
Oh, there was once   a   boat so   ve - ry   ti - ny,

Ha - bía u - na   vez   un   bar - co   chi - qui - ti - co,
Oh, there was once   a   boat so   ve - ry   ti - ny,

Que   no   po - dí - a,   que   no   po - dí - a,   que   no   po -
So   ve - ry   ti - ny,   so   ve - ry   ti - ny,   it   could   not

dí - a   na - ve - gar.   *Pa - sa - ron   u - na,   dos,   tres,*
e - ven   sail   a - way.   It   sat   for   one,   two,   three,   four,

Count and Sing

Before you **sing** the song, practice counting from one to seven
in Spanish: *uno, dos, tres, cuatro, cinco, seis, siete.*

cua - tro, cin - co, seis, sie - te se - ma - nas.
five, six, sev - en weeks there in the har - bor.

Pa - sa - ron u - na, dos, tres, cua - tro, cin - co,
It sat for one, two, three, four, five, six, sev - en

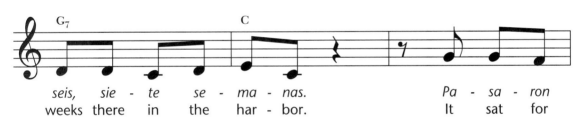

seis, sie - te se - ma - nas. Pa - sa - ron
weeks there in the har - bor. It sat for

u - na, dos, tres, cua - tro, cin - co, seis, sie - te se -
one, two, three, four, five, six, sev - en weeks there in the

ma - nas. Y el bar - qui - to, que no po -
har - bor. It was so ti - ny, so ve - ry

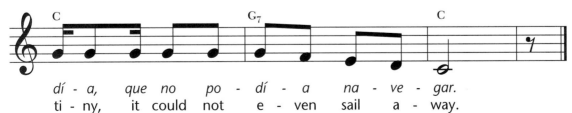

dí - a, que no po - dí - a na - ve - gar.
ti - ny, it could not e - ven sail a - way.

Rhythm Search

Look for these two rhythm patterns in *"El barquito."*

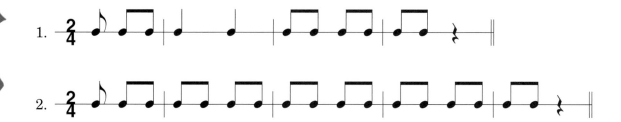

Now clap pattern 1, and pat pattern 2. Then **perform** the rhythm patterns as they occur in the song.

Move to the Rhythms

For the first half of the song, **move** with a partner. Using the pattern below, step, then clap your partner's hands. Then move in a circle for eight beats.

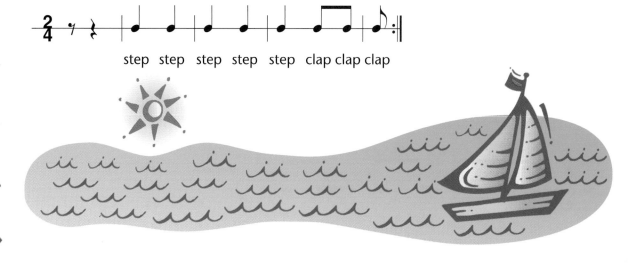

step   step   step   step   step   clap clap clap

Signing Away

Here's another way to perform this song. **Sing** the song, and use these hand signs.

uno
(one)

dos
(two)

tres
(three)

cuatro
(four)

cinco
(five)

seis
(six)

Listen for the percussion solo in this Latin American music.

11-12

Mambo Herd

by Tito Puente

Tito Puente [PWEHN-tay] made more than one hundred recordings of Latin American and swing music.

siete
(seven)

The Shape of Home

This is a song that tells a story about farm animals. What is the form of this song? **Sing** "Down Home." Then **create** your own verses to the song.

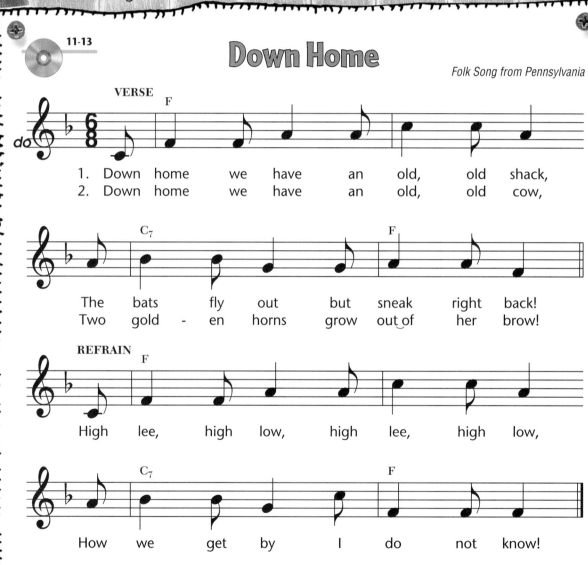

11-13

Down Home

Folk Song from Pennsylvania

VERSE F

1. Down home we have an old, old shack,
2. Down home we have an old, old cow,

C₇ ... F

The bats fly out but sneak right back!
Two gold - en horns grow out of her brow!

REFRAIN F

High lee, high low, high lee, high low,

C₇ ... F

How we get by I do not know!

3. Down home we have
   an old, old bull,
   He eats and eats
   and never gets full! *Refrain*

4. Down home we have
   an old, old goose,
   Her neck's a foot long and
   her feathers are loose! *Refrain*

Down Home with a Partner

For each verse, pantomime the animal with your partner. Then **move** on the refrain like this.

- Link right elbows and move in a circle on the first line of the refrain.

- Stamp your feet and flap your arms to the beat on the second line of the refrain.

Layers to Learn

This is a story from West Africa. Many cultures use stories to teach children the rules they should follow. **Listen** to "Zomo the Rabbit." What do you think is the lesson in this story?

11-15
Zomo the Rabbit

A Trickster Tale from West Africa

Zomo the Rabbit is one of many tricksters found in West African folk tales. Like all tricksters, clever Zomo outwits his larger foes.

In this story, Zomo wants to gain wisdom. The story begins with Zomo asking Sky God how he could become wise. Sky God tells Zomo that he must complete three almost impossible tasks. The story explains these tasks and how Zomo succeeds in his quest for wisdom.

Play with the Story

Learn to **play** this line of music.

Bass Xylophone

Now **play** this line to add another layer.

Alto Xylophone

Create a thicker texture by adding this line of music.

Soprano Xylophone

Tell Your Story

Retell the story of Zomo, using your own words.
Play these ostinatos together as a musical theme
between the sections of the story.

Video Library Watch *Storytelling*
to learn about different ways to tell a
story through music and movement.

Sing with a Spider

Music in movies is used to help tell the story. "We've Got Lots in Common" is from a movie you may know. **Sing** along with the animals in this song.

11-16

We've Got Lots in Common
from *Charlotte's Web*

Words and Music by Richard M. Sherman and Robert B. Sherman

1.   Oh, we've got   lots   in com-mon where it   real - ly counts,
2., 3. 'Cause we've got

Where it   real - ly counts, we've got   large   a - mounts.

What   we   look   like does - n't   count   an   ounce,

Last time to Coda ⊕

We've got lots   in   com-mon where it   real - ly counts.

(Wilbur) 2. You've

Another Song from a Story

Listen to *Colors of the Wind*, a song from another movie. What do the words tell you?

11-18
Colors of the Wind

**from *Pocahontas*
by Alan Menken and Stephen Schwartz**

This song is about appreciating the beauty in nature.

VERSE

(Wilbur) 1. You've got feath-ers, I've got skin, but both our out-sides hold us in.
got a beak and I've a snout, but both of us can sniff a-bout.

(Cow) I've got hooves, you've got webbed feet, but we both stand up to eat,
(Horse) You'll say "quack" and I'll say "neigh," but we're talk-ing ei-ther way,

⊕ *Coda*

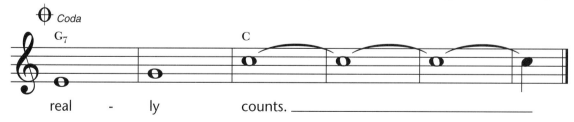

real - ly counts. _____

(Charlotte) 3. You're born to swim and me to spin,
but we all love this world we're in.
We share the sun, the earth, the sky
and that's the reason why
We've all got . . . *(D.S.)*

Tuneful Tales

ROCKIN' IN THE TREES

"Rockin' Robin" is an early rock and roll song. Imagine how it might feel to be a bird who could dance *and* fly!

Sing the song. For every verse, create a different steady-beat dance.

11-19

Rockin' Robin

Words and Music by Leon René

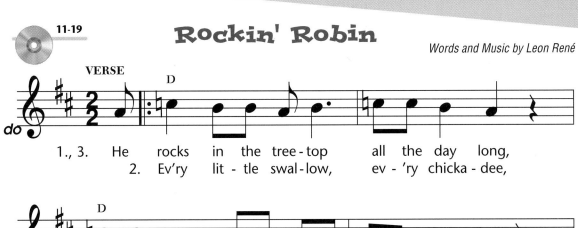

1., 3. He rocks in the tree-top all the day long,
2. Ev'ry lit-tle swal-low, ev-'ry chicka-dee,

Hop-pin' and a-bop-pin' and a-sing-in' his song.
Ev-'ry lit-tle bird __ in the tall __ oak tree. The

All the lit-tle birds on Jay - bird Street
wise __ old __ owl, on the big black crow,

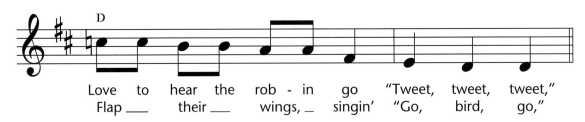

Love to hear the rob-in go "Tweet, tweet, tweet,"
Flap __ their __ wings, __ singin' "Go, bird, go,"

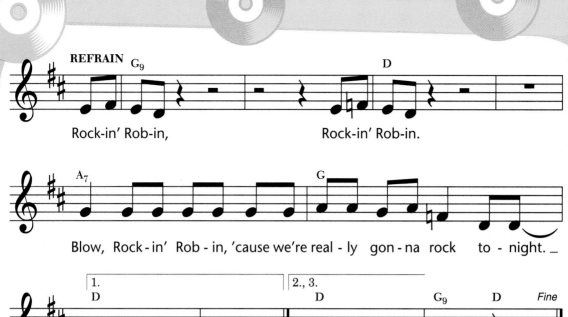

REFRAIN   G₉   D

Rock-in' Rob-in,   Rock-in' Rob-in.

A₇   G

Blow, Rock-in' Rob-in, 'cause we're real-ly gon-na rock to-night. __

1.   2., 3.
D   D   G₉   D   Fine

G

A pret-ty lit-tle ra-ven at the bird band-stand

D

Taught him how to do the bop and it was grand. They

G

start-ed go-in' stead-y, and bless my soul, He

A₇   *tacet*   *D.C. al Fine*

out-bopped the buz-zard and the o-ri-ole.

Web Site Go to *www.sbgmusic.com* to learn more about rock and roll music.

Tuneful Tales

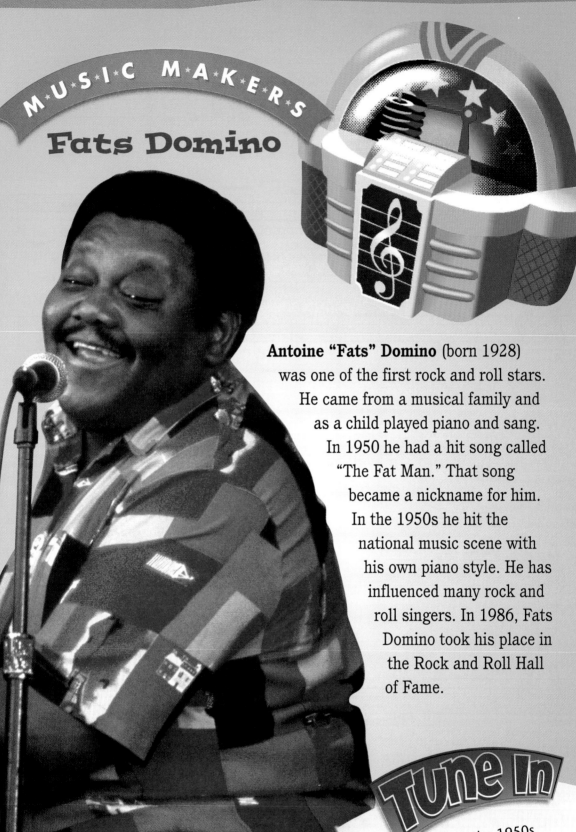

Fats Domino

Antoine "Fats" Domino (born 1928) was one of the first rock and roll stars. He came from a musical family and as a child played piano and sang. In 1950 he had a hit song called "The Fat Man." That song became a nickname for him. In the 1950s he hit the national music scene with his own piano style. He has influenced many rock and roll singers. In 1986, Fats Domino took his place in the Rock and Roll Hall of Fame.

Tune In

During the 1950s Fats Domino sold more records than any rock star except Elvis Presley.

Walk and Rock

Listen to Fats Domino perform *Walkin' to New Orleans.*
Follow the shape of the melody on the listening map.
What instruments do you recognize?

11-21

Walkin' to New Orleans

by Domino/Bartholomew/Guidry

This song is written in rock and roll style. How would you
describe its tempo?

Walkin' to New Orleans
Listening Map

Yes, I'm a walk- in' to New Or- leans.

I'm walk- in' to New Or- leans.

I'm gon- na need two pair of shoes

when I get through walkin' it blue.

When I get back to New Or- leans.

Tuneful Tales

Coats of Sound

This story song begins with a coat and ends with a button!
What happens? **Sing** the song to find out.

11-22

Words and Music by Paul Kaplan

1. I had an old coat, but the coat got torn.
2. Now, in a few years those __ threads got thin.

What - 'll I do? _____

I had an old coat, but the coat got torn.
Now, in a few years those __ threads got thin.

What - 'll I do? _____

I had an old coat, but the coat got torn.
Now, in a few years those __ threads got thin.

Move Like a Coat!

As you sing the song, **move** to show how the coat changes.

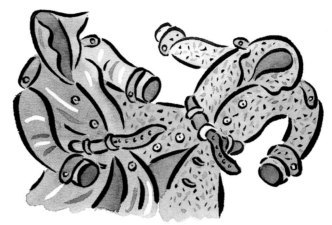

So I   cut   it   down and a   jack - et   was   born.
So I   called it a   shirt and I   tucked _ it   in.

And   I   sing   ev - 'ry day _   of   my   life. _____

3. The sleeves wore out in the east and west. What'll I do? *(2 times)*
   The sleeves wore out in the east and west, So I pulled them off and I had a vest.
   And I sing. . .

4. I stained that vest with cherry pie. What'll I do? *(2 times)*
   I stained that vest with cherry pie, So I cut and sewed 'til I had me a tie.
   And I sing. . .

5. Now, when that tie was a-lookin' lean. What'll I do? *(2 times)*
   Now, when that tie was a-lookin' lean, I made a patch for my old blue-jeans.
   And I sing. . .

6. Well, when that patch was next to nothin'. What'll I do? *(2 times)*
   Well, when that patch was next to nothin', I rolled it up into a button.
   And I'll sing. . .

7. Well, when that button was almost gone. What'll I do? *(2 times)*
   Well, when that button was almost gone, With what was left I made this song.
   And I'll sing. . .

Tuneful Tales

Celebrations!

Sing "Let's Celebrate," a song for any holiday.

Holidays to Share

All through the year, there's something to celebrate!

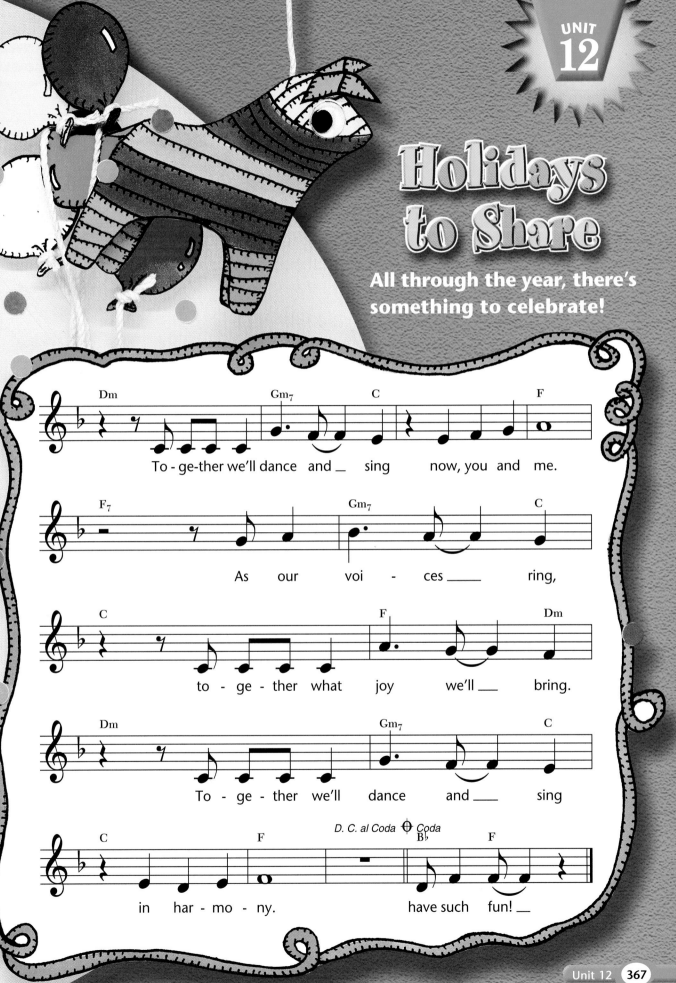

To - ge-ther we'll dance and _ sing now, you and me.

As our voi - ces _____ ring,

to - ge - ther what joy we'll __ bring.

To - ge - ther we'll dance and ___ sing

D. C. al Coda ✛ *Coda*

in har - mo - ny.

have such fun! __

United in Peace

Celebration songs are used for many reasons. *"Hevenu shalom aleichem"* is a song that celebrates peace. **Move** to show same and different phrases as you **sing** the song.

11-25

Hevenu shalom aleichem
(We Come to Greet You in Peace)

Hebrew Folk Song

He - ve - nu sha - lom a - lei - chem, He - ve - nu
We come to greet you in peace, ___ We come to

sha - lom a - lei - chem, He - ve - nu sha - lom a -
greet you in peace, ___ We come to greet ___ you in

lei - chem, He - ve - nu sha - lom, sha - lom,
peace, ___ We come to greet you, greet you,

1.   2.

sha - lom a - lei - chem. He - ve - nu sha - lom a - lei - chem.
greet ___ you in peace. We come to greet ___ you in peace.

▲ United Nations Building, New York City

Show Your Colors!

In 1945, fifty-one countries joined together to form the United Nations. The goal of the United Nations is peace through cooperation. Today more than 180 countries belong to the United Nations. Each nation has a flag flying at the U.N.

Listen to *Common Ground*. It celebrates the environment. The composer was honored for his contribution to environmental causes.

11-29

Common Ground

**from *Concert for the Earth*
by Ivan Lins
as performed by
the Paul Winter Consort**

Common Ground was recorded live at the United Nations Assembly Hall.

Paul Winter playing ▶
a soprano saxophone

Pumpkin Time!

Have you ever been in a pumpkin patch? If so, you know that pumpkins grow on vines. They can be used for pies, decorations, or jack-o-lanterns. **Sing** this pumpkin patch song.

11-30

In the Pumpkin Patch

Words and Music by Elizabeth Gilpatrick

1. When I grew up in the pump - kin patch,

I sat in the sun all day.

I grew 'til I was gold and round,

Then I heard a lit - tle sun - beam say:

2. "Roll around, little pumpkin in the pumpkin patch;
   Oh, tumble and turn and sway.
   Roll around in the grasses and the weeds and the thatch,
   Oh, spin and roll and play.

3. "But when the sun is sinking low
   And shadows steal the light,
   Hurry back to your home in the garden row;
   Curl up in your vines so tight."

Pumpkin Rhythms

Read the rhythms of "In the Pumpkin Patch." Tap and say the rhythm for each phrase of the song.

Read this poem. Then **create** ostinatos to accompany it.

Pumpkin Poem

Author Unknown

One day I found two pumpkin seeds.

I planted one and pulled the weeds.

It sprouted roots and a big, long vine.

A pumpkin grew; I called it mine.

The pumpkin was quite round and fat.

(I really am quite proud of that.)

But there is something I'll admit

That has me worried just a bit.

I ate the other seed, you see.

Now will it grow inside of me?

(I'm so relieved since I have found

That pumpkins only grow in the ground!)

A Tricky Song

On Halloween, you might see people dressed in unusual costumes. Or you might wear an unusual costume yourself! **Listen** to "Halloween Is a Very Unusual Night." What unusual things are mentioned in this song?

12-1

Halloween Is a Very Unusual Night

Words and Music by Ned Ginsburg

VERSE

1. There's on-ly one night like this all year,
2. Drop __ your fears and off you go,

On-ly one night when spi-rits ap-pear;
Join __ the tra-veling cos-tume show. __

An eve-ning meant to be spent out-side,
Grab your sack and at-tack the street,

Yes, it's Hal-lo-ween, and you can-not hide.
But you bet-ter start to __ trick-or-treat.

Catch a Rhythm

Clap the rhythm patterns of the refrain as you **sing** the song. Then **create** your own rhythm ostinatos to accompany the song.

When the ghosts come out, and the gob-lins creep,

and the skel-e-tons rat-tle. How could an - y - bod - y sleep?

And the mon-sters march, while the witch-es take flight.

Yes, Hal - lo-ween is a ver-y un-u - su-al night!

Yes, Hal - lo-ween is a ver-y un-u - su-al night!

Head for Thanksgiving

Thanksgiving is a time for getting together with family and friends. **Sing** this traditional song about Thanksgiving.

12-3

Over the River and Through the Wood

Words by Lydia Maria Child

Traditional

do

1. O - ver the riv - er and through the wood,

To Grand - fa - ther's house we go; _____

The horse knows the way to car - ry the sleigh

Through the white and drift - ed snow. _____

O - ver the riv - er and through the wood,

Oh, how the wind does blow! _____

Arts Connection

Freedom from Want
by Norman Rockwell (1894–1978)
This painting is one of a series
called *The Four Freedoms.* ▶
Rockwell was famous for painting
pictures of everyday American life.

It stings the toes and bites the nose

As o - ver the ground we go.

2. Over the river and through the wood,
   Trot fast, my dapple gray!
   Spring over the ground like a
     hunting hound,
   For this is Thanksgiving Day!

Over the river and through the wood,
Now Grandmother's face I spy!
Hurrah for the fun! Is the
  pudding done?
Hurrah for the pumpkin pie!

Winter Weather Music

In some parts of the world, winter is so cold, you can see your breath in the air! What happens when winter arrives in your town? **Sing** this winter song in unison. Then sing it in canon.

12-5

Knock No More

Words and Music by Elizabeth Gilpatrick

I
When Old Man Win-ter ___ comes knock-ing at your door,

II
he'll nip your fin-gers ___ and freeze you to the core.

III
Knock! Knock! Can't come in! Knock no more!

Play in Winter

Learn to **play** these ostinatos to accompany "Knock No More." What happens to the texture of the song when each ostinato is added?

Create Winter Music

Read "Dragon Smoke," then **create** a rhythm ostinato to go with it.

Dragon Smoke

by Lilian Moore

Breathe and blow
white clouds
    with every puff.

It's cold today
    cold enough
to see your breath.

Huff!
    Breathe dragon smoke
      today!

Sing for Chanukah

A dreydl is a spinning top that is used in Chanukah games. There are four symbols on the dreydl—*nun, gimel, hay,* and *shin.*

Listen to "Chanukah Games." What do the four symbols mean in the game?

Holiday Melody

Look at the song. Find a place where the melody moves by skip. Find a place where the melody moves by step. Which measures are the same?

Sing "Chanukah Games." Sing the octaves smoothly.

Chanukah Games

Words by Rose C. Engel and Judith M. Berman

Music by Judith M. Berman

1. Cha - nu - kah's the time for games. Read - y, now be - gin!
2. Round and round the drey - dl goes, See it hop and run.

Spin your drey - dl, let it go, Ev - 'ry - one join in.
When at last it stops on *nun,* Priz - es? Not a one.

Spin your drey - dl, let it go, Ev - 'ry - one join in!
When at last it stops on *nun,* Priz - es? Not a one.

REFRAIN

Nun and *gi - mel, hay* and *shin,* Los - er, win - ner, spin and spin!

3. In a circle, dreydl, turn, turn and slowly sway.
   If you stop on *gimel* now, I win all—Hooray!
   If you stop on *gimel* now, I win all—Hooray! *Refrain*

4. Funny little dreydl top, how you make me laugh!
   But if now you stop on *hay,* I take only half!
   But if now you stop on *hay,* I take only half! *Refrain*

5. Whirling, twirling, dreydl, go, on one foot you dance;
   Shin says I must put one in and take another chance!
   Shin says I must put one in and take another chance! *Refrain*

Holidays to Share

Eight Days to Celebrate

Keep the beat while you **sing** "Hanuka, Hanuka."

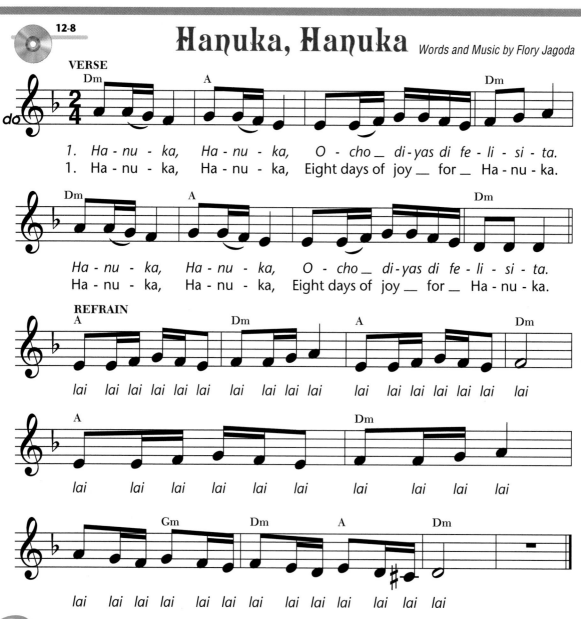

12-8

Hanuka, Hanuka

Words and Music by Flory Jagoda

VERSE

Dm   A   Dm

do

1. Ha - nu - ka, Ha - nu - ka, O - cho __ di - yas di fe - li - si - ta.
1. Ha - nu - ka, Ha - nu - ka, Eight days of joy __ for __ Ha - nu - ka.

Dm   A   Dm

Ha - nu - ka, Ha - nu - ka, O - cho __ di - yas di fe - li - si - ta.
Ha - nu - ka, Ha - nu - ka, Eight days of joy __ for __ Ha - nu - ka.

REFRAIN

A   Dm   A   Dm

lai lai lai lai lai lai   lai   lai lai lai   lai   lai lai lai lai lai   lai

A   Dm

lai   lai   lai   lai   lai   lai   lai   lai   lai   lai

Gm   Dm   A   Dm

lai   lai lai lai lai   lai lai lai   lai lai lai   lai lai lai

380

The Way to Celebrate

Chanukah celebrations include singing, dancing, and playing games. One candle is lit on each of the eight nights of Chanukah.

Holiday Listening

Describe the melody of this funny Chanukah song.

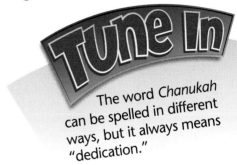

The word *Chanukah* can be spelled in different ways, but it always means "dedication."

12-12
The Dreydl Song

Traditional Hebrew

You can make up your own verses to this song about making dreydls.

2. *Hanuka, Hanuka,*
   Ocho diyas de kantar.
   Hanuka, Hanuka,
   Ocho diyas de kantar.
   Refrain

3. *Hanuka, Hanuka,*
   Ocho diyas de bayar.
   Hanuka, Hanuka,
   Ocho diyas de bayar.
   Refrain

4. *Hanuka, Hanuka,*
   Ocho diyas de guzar.
   Hanuka, Hanuka,
   Ocho diyas de guzar.
   Refrain

2. Hanuka, Hanuka,
   Eight days of singing for Hanuka.
   Everyone sing, let voices ring,
   Eight days of singing for Hanuka.
   Refrain

3. Hanuka, Hanuka,
   Eight days of dancing for Hanuka.
   Raise arms high, let feet fly,
   Eight days of dancing for Hanuka.
   Refrain

4. Hanuka, Hanuka,
   Eight happy days of Hanuka.
   Play, dance, and sing, let voices ring,
   Eight happy days of Hanuka.
   Refrain

Holidays to Share

An Add-On Spiritual

"Children, Go Where I Send Thee" is a Christmas spiritual.
Create a way to **move** for each verse of this add-on song.

12-13
Children, Go Where I Send Thee

African American Spiritual

1. Chil-dren, go where I send thee; How shall I send thee?

I will send thee one by one. ___

Well, one was the lit-tle bit-ty ba - by, ___

Wrapped in swad - dling cloth - ing, ___

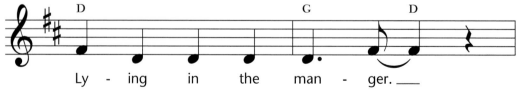

Ly - ing in the man - ger. ___

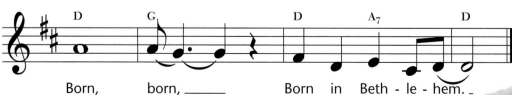

Born, born, ___ Born in Beth - le - hem. _

A Mountaintop Christmas

Listen for the verse and refrain in another Christmas spiritual.

12-15
Go, Tell It on the Mountain

Traditional African American

This version is sung by the
Booker T. Washington Singers.

2. Children, go where I send thee;
    How shall I send thee?
    I will send thee two by two.
    Well, two was the Paul and Silas,
    One was the little bitty baby,
    Wrapped in swaddling clothing,
    Lying in the manger.
    Born, born,
    Born in Bethlehem.

3. . . . I will send thee three by three.
    Well, three was the three men riding,
    Two was the Paul and Silas, . . .

4. . . . I will send thee four by four.
    Well, four was the four come a-knocking at the door,
    Three was the three men riding, . . .

5. . . . I will send thee five by five.
    Well, five was the Gospel preachers,
    Four was the four come a-knocking at the door, . . .

6. . . . I will send thee six by six.
    Well, six was the six that couldn't be fixed,
    Five was the Gospel preachers, . . .

7. . . . I will send thee seven by seven.
    Well, seven was the seven who went to heaven,
    Six was the six that couldn't be fixed, . . .

8. . . . I will send thee eight by eight.
    Well, eight was the eight who stood by the gate,
    Seven was the seven who went to heaven, . . .

9. . . . I will send thee nine by nine.
    Well, nine was the nine who saw the sign,
    Eight was the eight who stood by the gate, . . .

10. . . . I will send thee ten by ten.
    Well, ten was the Ten Commandments,
    Nine was the nine who saw the sign, . . .

Holidays to Share

Christmas in Many Places

Here's a Jamaican Christmas song with words you might not know. *Lama* is the Jamaican word for presents. *Deggeday* is the word for dress-up clothes. **Sing** "Chrismus a Come."

12-16

Chrismus a Come

Traditional Song from Jamaica

Chris - mus a come, me wan __ me la - ma,

Chris - mus a come, me wan __ me la - ma,

Chris - mus a come, me wan __ me deg - ge - day,

Chris - mus a come, me wan __ me deg - ge - day.

Christmas Beat

Now **play** this ostinato to accompany "Chrismus a Come." Tap and say the rhythm, then play it.

It's Almost Here!

Sometimes it's hard to wait for a special holiday. **Sing** along with "Almost Day," a song about waiting for Christmas. Then **create** your own ostinato to accompany the song.

Almost Day

Folk Song from the United States

1. Chick-ens crow-in' for mid-night, it's al-most day,
Refrain: Chick-ens crow-in' for mid-night, it's al-most day.

Chick-ens crow-in' for mid-night, it's al-most day.
Chick-ens crow-in' for mid-night, it's al-most day.

2. Santa Claus is comin', it's almost day. . .
Refrain

3. Think I heard my ma say it's almost day. . .
Refrain

4. Think I heard my pa say it's almost day. . .
Refrain

© by Huddie Ledbetter, Folkways Music Publisherss, 1959.

Holidays to Share

Posada, Piñata, Presents

Las posadas is part of the Christmas celebration in Mexico. Children carry small religious figures from house to house. Then they have a party with a *piñata* game. A *piñata* is a papier-mâché figure with candy and toys inside. **Move** to show the tempo changes in *"La piñata"* as you play the game.

La piñata

English Words by Alice Firgau   *Folk Song from Mexico*

VERSE

1. En las no-ches de   po - sa - das, La pi - ña-ta es lo me - jor: _____
1. On po - sa - da nights we have such fun, The *pi - ña - ta* is the best of all.

Aun las ni - ñas re - mil - ga - das Se an-i - man con gran fer - vor.
E - ven shy girls join with   ev - 'ry - one As we try to make it   fall.

REFRAIN

Da - le,   da - le,   da - le,   no pier - das   el   ti - no.
There's the big *pi - ña - ta*,   See if you can whack it,

Mi - de   la   dis - tan - cia   que hay en   el   ca - mi - no.
Turn and swing, you'll hit   it,   Hit   it   hard, you'll crack   it.

Que si no le das de un pa - lo te em - pi - no,
And   if you don't break it, I'll raise you up there like   it,

¡Por - que tie - nes au - ra de pu - ro pe - pi - no!
Like   a big *pi - ña - ta*. So you bet - ter strike   it!

2. Con tus ojitos vendados
    Y en las manos un bastón;
    ¡La olla rómpela a pedazos!
    ¡No le tengas compasión!
    Refrain

2. Put a blindfold over both your eyes,
    Take a stick in both your hands.
    Break the pot and let the pieces fly!
    Show no mercy, that's the plan!
    Refrain

Holiday Happenings

"*Aguinaldo*" is a Puerto Rican carol that is sung as children go from house to house during festival days after Christmas. **Listen** to the song, then **sing** along.

12-24

Aguinaldo

English Words courtesy of
CP Language Institute, New York

Carol from Puerto Rico

VERSE

1. Á - bre-me la puer - ta   Á - bre-me la puer - ta
1. O-pen up the front door,   O-pen up the front door,

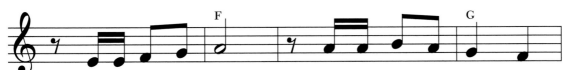

Que lo quie - ro en - trar;   He he-cho mis pas - te - les
Let me en - ter in.   I have made pas - te - les

Y no quier - en que dar. ____   He he-cho mis pas - te - les
For my friends with - in. ____   I have made pas - te - les

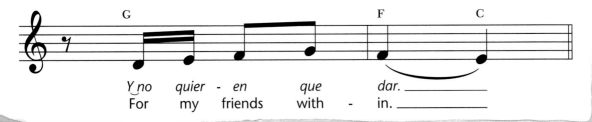

Y no quier - en que dar. ____
For my friends with - in. ____

388

Play for the Holiday

Create ostinatos to add more layers of sound to *"Aguinaldo."*
Use these instruments.

REFRAIN

A la sa - len - de - ra,
Oh, what joy I'm feel - ing,

A la sa - len - de - ra,
Oh, what joy I'm feel - ing,

A la sa - len - de - ra,
Oh, what joy I'm feel - ing

de mi co - ra - zón.
deep with-in my heart.

2. *Si no tiene nada*
    Si no tiene nada
    Nada nos dará;
    Pero lo que queremos
    cariño y bondad.
    Pero lo que queremos
    cariño y bondad.
    Refrain

2. If you've no possessions,
    If you've no possessions,
    Nothing can you share,
    But give love and kindness,
    Gifts beyond compare,
    But give love and kindness,
    Gifts beyond compare.
    Refrain

Kwanzaa!

During *Kwanzaa* [KWAHN-zah], some African American families gather to celebrate their African heritage. They greet each other by saying *"Habari Gani."* These words are Swahili for "What's the news?" or "What's happening?" Identify skips in the song. Then **sing** *"Habari Gani."*

12-28

Habari Gani

Words and Music by James McBride

1. Win - ter ___ is here, so *Kwan - zaa* ___ is near, Cel - e -
2. Peace be ___ un - to you, good things come true When you

brat - ing joy and love   as a hap - py fam - i - ly.
spread your joy and love   in a hap - py fam - i - ly.

Join us in our greet - ing with sev - en days of hol - i - day,
Self - de - ter - mi - na - tion, ___ liv - ing as a na - tion, too.

Shar - ing all our gifts and love in a hap - py gath - er - ing.
We're all one re - la - tion and ___ live in har - mo - ny.

What's the Answer?

During *Kwanzaa,* there are special answers to the question *"Habari Gani"?* The answer is different for each of the seven days and nights of the celebration.

Umoja [oo-MOE-jah]	Unity
Kujichagulia [koo-jee-cha-goo-LEE-ah]	Self-determination
Ujima [oo-JEE-mah]	Collective work and responsibility
Ujamaa [oo-JAH-mah]	Sharing
Nia [nee-AH]	Purpose
Kuumba [koo-OOM-bah]	Creativity
Imani [ee-MAH-nee]	Faith

Hap-py *Kwan-zaa!* Hap-py *Kwan-zaa!* Love and peace ___ from me to you. *Ha-ba-ri Ga-ni* spreads the news ___ of joy to you and asks "What's new?" new?" new?" "What's new?" *Ha-ba-ri Ga-ni!*

Happy New Year!

New Year's Day in Japan is a time for visiting friends and relatives. People wish each other good luck and send good luck cards. New Year's Day celebrations include music festivals. **Listen** for the timbre of Japanese instruments in *"Ichi-gatsu tsuitachi."*

13-1

Ichi-gatsu tsuitachi
(A New Year's Greeting)

Words by Senge Takatomi
English Words Adapted by Katherine S. Bolt

Music by Ue Sanemichi
School Song from Japan

と　し　の　は　じ　め　の　た　め　し　と　て
To - shi - no ha - ji - me no Ta - me - shi to - te
"O - me - de - to go - zai - mas," we will bow and say,

お　わ　り　な　き　よ　の　め　で　た　さ　を
O - wa - ri na - ki yo no Me - de - ta - sa o
"O - me - de - to go - zai - mas," Hap - py New Year's Day.

Tune In

At midnight on New Year's Day, temple gongs in Japan are rung 108 times to chase away greed.

Listen to this song played on Japanese instruments. It is a duet for *koto* [KOH-toh] and *shakuhachi* [shah-koo-HAH-chee].

13-5
Yamaji

by Kozo Masuda

This piece represents the composer's view of the Japanese countryside.

まつ　た　け　た　て　て　か　ど　ご　と　に
Mat - su - ta - ke ta - te te Ka - do go - to ni
Let us place our pine branch-es here be-side the door,

い　おう＿　きょう＿　こ　そ　た　の　し　け　れ
I - wo ＿ kyo ＿ ko - so Ta - no - shi - ke - re.
And wish our friends and neigh-bors man - y new years more.

Holidays to Share

Honoring a King

"Keep Your Eyes on the Prize" is a song from the civil rights movement of the 1960s. Think about what the prize is while you **sing** this song.

Keep Your Eyes on the Prize

African American Freedom Song

13-6

do

	Cm		Fm	Cm

1. Got my hand on the free - dom plow,
2. We fought jail and ___ vio - lence too,

	Cm		Fm	Cm

Won't give no - thin' for my jour - ney now.
But God's love ___ has ___ seen us through.

	Cm		G₇	Cm

Keep your eyes on ___ the prize. Hold on!

394

An American Hero

Martin Luther King, Jr., fought for equal rights for African American people. He led non-violent protests and made speeches to inspire the civil rights movement.

Many songs have been written about Martin Luther King. **Listen** for the message of hope in *Shed a Little Light*.

13-7
Shed a Little Light

by James Taylor

In this song, Martin Luther King's message is the "light" that helps us see how we can work together for freedom and equality.

▲ In 1964, Martin Luther King, Jr., received the Nobel Peace Prize for his leadership.

3. Work all day and work all night,
   Tryin' to gain our civil rights.
   Keep your eyes on the prize.
   Hold on! *Refrain*

4. The only chain that a man can stand
   Is the chain of a hand in hand.
   Keep your eyes on the prize.
   Hold on! *Refrain*

Holidays to Share

Sing for Right

Before the civil rights movement, African Americans in some communities were not allowed to sit together with white people on buses. One day Rosa Parks, an African American woman, refused to move from the front of the bus to the back. Her example helped others have the courage to fight for their rights as American citizens.

Sing this song that honors Rosa Parks.

Back of the Bus

13-8

Traditional Song
Adapted by Miss Mary Jane Pigee

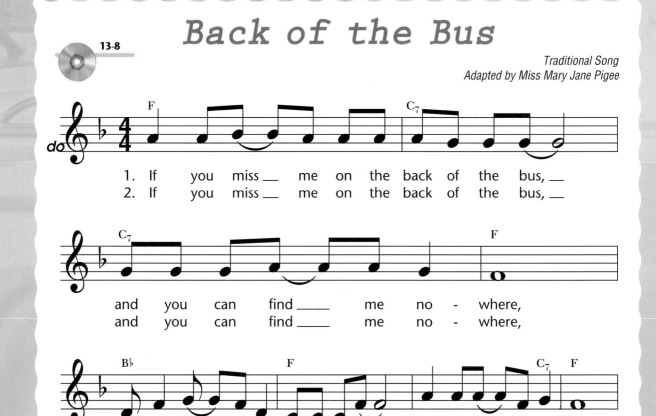

1. If you miss me on the back of the bus, —
2. If you miss me on the back of the bus, —

and you can find me no - where,
and you can find me no - where,

Come on up to the front of the bus, — I'll be rid - in' up there.
Come on up to the driv - er's seat, — I'll be driv - ing there.

I'll be rid - in' up there, I'll be rid - in' up there.
I'll be driv - ing there, I'll be driv - ing there.

Come on up __ to the front of the bus, __ I'll be rid - in' up there.
Come on up __ to the driv - er's seat, __ I'll be driv - ing there.

A Musical Tribute

Listen to *Sister Rosa.* How do the performers use *staccato* and *legato* sounds to create a sense of pride?

13-10
Sister Rosa

by the Neville Brothers

The Neville Brothers use rap style in this tribute to Rosa Parks.

Sing of Liberty!

What does *liberty* mean? Look for clues as you **sing** this patriotic song.

13-11

America

Words by Samuel Francis Smith   *Traditional Melody*

1. My coun - try! 'tis of thee, Sweet land of lib - er - ty,
2. My na - tive coun - try, thee, Land of the no - ble free,
3. Let mu - sic swell the breeze, And ring from all the trees

Of thee I sing; Land where my fa - thers died,
Thy name I sing; I love thy rocks and rills,
Sweet Free - dom's song; Let mor - tal tongues a - wake,

Land of the Pil - grims' pride, From ev - 'ry ____
Thy woods and tem - pled hills; My heart __ with __
Let all that breathe par - take. Let rocks __ their __

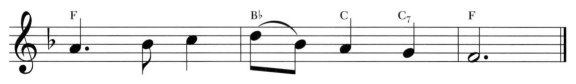

moun - tain - side Let ____ free - dom ring!
rap - ture thrills Like ____ that a - bove.
si - lence break, The ____ sound pro - long.

"America, the Beautiful" is a song celebrating the beauty of our country. How would you describe the tempo of this song?

America, the Beautiful

Words by Katharine Lee Bates

Music by Samuel A. Ward

1. O beau-ti-ful for spa-cious skies, For am-ber waves of grain,
2. O beau-ti-ful for pa-triot dream That sees be-yond the years

For pur-ple moun-tain maj-es-ties A-bove the fruit-ed plain!
Thine al-a-bas-ter cit-ies gleam, Un-dimmed by hu-man tears!

A-mer-i-ca! A-mer-i-ca! God shed His grace on thee,

And crown thy good with broth-er-hood From sea to shin-ing sea!

Listen to this version of *America, the Beautiful.* How is it different from the first version you heard?

America, the Beautiful

by Katherine Lee Bates and Samuel A. Ward

This version of *America the Beautiful* is sung in

Holidays to Share

Yankee Doodle Days

Patriotic songs celebrate our country. **Move** to show the meter of "Yankee Doodle." Then **sing** it for fun!

13-16

Yankee Doodle

Words by Dr. Richard Shuckburgh   *Traditional*

1.   ⸠ Fath'r and I went down to camp, A - long with Cap - tain Good-in',
2.   And there we saw a   thou-sand men, As   rich as   Squire __ Da - vid;

And there we saw the men and boys As thick as hast - y pud - din'.
And what they wast-ed ev - 'ry day, I   wish it could be sav - ed.

Yan - kee Doo - dle, keep it   up,   Yan - kee Doo - dle dan - dy,

Mind   the mu - sic   and the   step And with the girls be hand - y.

3.   And there was Captain Washington
     Upon a slapping stallion,
     A-giving orders to his men;
     I guess there was a million. *Refrain*

Sing About Our Flag

Sing "The Star-Spangled Banner," our national anthem.

The Star-Spangled Banner

Words by Francis Scott Key   *Music by John Stafford Smith*

Playing the Recorder

Getting Ready

This section of your book will help you learn to **play** the soprano recorder, a small wind instrument.

To get started, try this trick!
- Extend your hand forward with palm upward.
- Pretend you have a small feather on your palm.
- Blow the feather gently so it moves across your palm without falling.

This is all the air you need to produce a good sound.

Covering the Holes

Using your left hand, cover the holes shown in the picture. Be sure to press just hard enough so that the holes make a light mark on your fingers. Remove your hand to check that there is an outline of a circle on each finger. Hold the bottom of the recorder with your right hand, balancing it with your thumb and pinky. Don't cover the bottom holes.

G

Let's Play G

Put your hands in position to play G. Cover the tip of the mouthpiece with your lips. Blow gently as you whisper *daah*. Practice playing G using a steady beat pattern of quarter notes.

Play this pattern throughout the verse of "Li'l Liza Jane" (page 136).

Patterns on G

Play this ostinato throughout "*Kum bachur atzel*" (page 134). Whisper *daah* on each note so you can hear a short–short–long pattern.

Adding A

Look at the diagrams for G and A. Try playing G for four beats followed by four beats of A. When you uncover the third hole, what happens to the sound of your recorder?

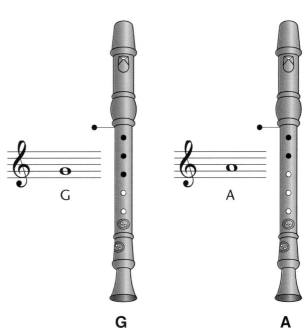

Playing A and G

You are now ready to **play** a **countermelody** during the verses of "Old Dan Tucker" (page 92).

A **countermelody** is a different melody that is played or sung at the same time as the main melody.

Ready for B

Now you are ready to learn to **play** B. Cover the holes shown in the diagram. Will B sound higher or lower than G and A?

B

B

Here is a recorder part that you can play while others sing "*Ahora voy a cantarles*" (page 52).

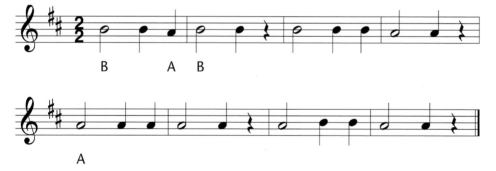

"B-A-G" Songs

Now that you can play B, A, and G, you will be able to **play** "Frog in the Millpond" (page 12) and "Hot Cross Buns" (page 214).

Building Right Hand Strength

Here are two new notes. Cover the holes securely with your fingers flat, not arched, and whisper *daah*. Be sure to have your left hand on the top and the right hand below.

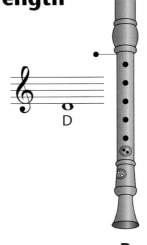

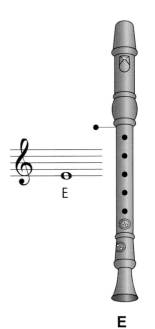

D   **E**

Now you are ready to **play** a countermelody to accompany the singing of "*Piñon, pirulín.*" Make sure you observe each quarter rest.

D   E

Recorder Long Ago

The lute and recorder were instruments heard in the royal courts of Europe beginning in the late 1400s or early 1500s.

Listen to *Sonata Seconda*. Is the recorder playing mostly long or mostly short sounds?

13-20
Sonata Seconda

by Dario Castello

This piece is played on soprano recorder and lute. It was written in the 1600s.

Mallet Instruments

Many Mallets to Choose

Mallets are percussion sticks with different types of ends. Some ends are wrapped with yarn, some are hard wood, plastic, hard rubber, or metal. The type of mallet you use to play an instrument will affect its timbre.

Since glockenspiels have a high, bright sound, you can use wooden-ended mallets to produce a warm, clear sound.

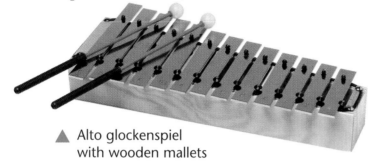

▲ Alto glockenspiel with wooden mallets

Sound Choices

Xylophones and metallophones can be played with either soft-ended or hard-ended mallets, depending on the type of sound you want to produce. What kind of sound do you think a hard-ended mallet will make?

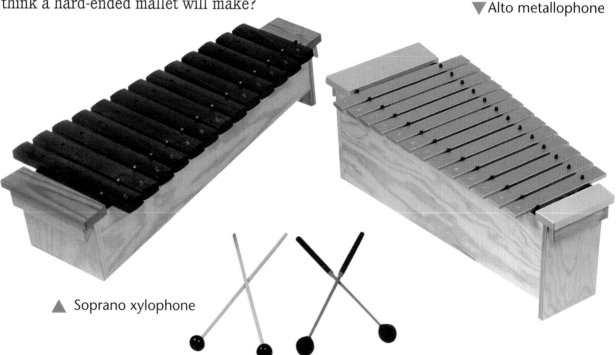

▼ Alto metallophone

▲ Soprano xylophone

Be careful to choose mallets that are the right size for the instrument. If the bars bounce when you strike them, the mallets are probably too large.

Bass xylophone ▶

Time to Play!

Play this **bordun** on the alto xylophone. What kind of mallet will you choose?

A **bordun** is a repeated pattern used to accompany music. It has two pitches, one of which is the home tone.

Be sure to hold the mallets with a relaxed grip.

Sound Bank

◀ **Bagpipe** A wind instrument in which one or more pipes are attached to a windbag. One or two of the pipes, called chanters, have finger holes and can play a melody. The other pipes, called drones, sound single pitches. p. 35 CD 13-21

◀ *Caja* [KAH-hah] A short, squat drum made from a hollow log, with two drumheads. The player uses two sticks to strike one head and the side of the drum. The drum is often placed on the ground and held with one foot while the performer plays. p. 265 CD 13-22

◀ **Cello** [CHEH-loh] A large wooden string instrument. The cello may be plucked with fingers or played with a bow. The cello has a rich, warm voice that can sound quite low. p. 34 CD 13-23

◀ **Clarinet** An instrument shaped like a long cylinder. It is usually made of wood with a reed in the mouthpiece. The clarinet's low notes are soft and hollow. The highest notes are thin and piercing. p. 20 CD 13-24

◀ **Conga** [KAHN-gah] An Afro-Cuban drum with a long barrel-shaped body. It comes in two sizes: the small quinto and the large tumbador. The conga is struck with the fingers and the palms of the hands. p. 36 CD 13-25

Instrument Key: strings percussion woodwind brass

◀ **Flute** A small, metal instrument shaped like a pipe. The player holds the flute sideways and blows across an open mouthpiece. The flute's voice is clear and sweet. p. 180
CD 13-26

◀ **Flute (Native American)** An end-blown instrument made from a wooden tube. Part of the upper end of the tube is cut out to make the sound. Finger holes along the body help the player change pitches. This flute sounds very much like a recorder. p. 249 CD 13-27

◀ **French Horn** A medium-sized instrument made of coiled brass tubing. At one end is a large bell; at the other end is a mouthpiece. The sound of the horn is mellow and warm. p. 185 CD 13-28

◀ **Guitar** A wooden instrument with six nylon or steel strings. The player strums or plucks the strings with a pick or the fingers. You can use a guitar to play a melody. You can also play chords to accompany a melody. p. 71 CD 13-29

◀ *Guitarrón* [gee-tah-ROHN] A large bass guitar with a round back. It is strung with six harp strings and is played in Mexican *mariachi* groups. p. 312 CD 13-30

Sound Bank

Most instruments appear on the page indicated. In a few instances, the reference is to a family of instruments.

 **Harpsichord** A keyboard instrument shaped like a piano. When the keys are pressed, the strings inside the instrument are plucked by small quills. This gives the sound a tinkling quality. p. 209 CD 13-31

Irish Harp A small, triangular-shaped stringed instrument. The strings are made of brass or gut. They are strummed or plucked. p. 285 CD 13-32

Jarana [ha-RAH-nah] An eight-string guitar used in folk music of Mexico. It is strummed or plucked with the fingers. p. 246 CD 13-33

 **Koto** [KOH-toh] A Japanese string instrument with seven to seventeen long strings. These are set high above the body of the instrument, which sits flat on the floor. The sound is a little like that of a harp. p. 393 CD 13-34

Marimba A large, barred instrument played with mallets. The bars are made of rosewood, with long resonating tubes that hang below each bar. The marimba has a mellow ringing sound. p. 146 CD 13-35

Panpipes A wind instrument that consists of a set of hollow tubes of different lengths tied together. Sound is produced by blowing across the open upper ends. Each tube has its own pitch. The longer the tube, the lower its pitch. p. 180 CD 13-36

◀ **Piano** A large keyboard instrument with strings inside. When the keys are pressed, hammers in the piano hit the strings to make them sound. p. 324 CD 13-37

◀ *Pujador* [POO-hah-dohr] A medium-sized drum from Panama. It has one drumhead, and is held between the knees and hit with the hands. p. 265 CD 13-38

◀ *Repicador* [reh-PEEK-ah-dohr] A small drum from Panama. It is tapered, with one drumhead. It is held between the knees and hit with the hands. p. 265 CD 13-39

◀ *Requinto* [reh-KEEN-toh] A small guitar similar to a ukulele. It has four strings that are plucked with a long, thin pick. The requinto often plays very fast melodies. p. 247 CD 13-40

◀ *Shakuhachi* [shah-koo-HAH-chee] A Japanese flute made of bamboo. The *shakuhachi* is played with lots of pitch bends, clicks, and flutters. It sounds like a human singing voice and can produce unusual, airy sounds. p. 180 CD 13-41

Sound Bank

Most instruments appear on the page indicated. In a few instances, the reference is to a family of instruments.

◀ **Snare Drum** A small, cylinder-shaped drum with two heads. Snares, or strings wrapped with wire, are stretched across the bottom head to create a vibrating sound. A snare drum can make a long, raspy roll or a sharp, rhythmic beating sound. p. 400 CD 13-42

◀ **String Bass** A large, wooden string instrument that is either plucked or bowed. The string bass is so tall that the player must stand up or sit on a high stool to play it. The voice of the string bass is deep, dark, and sometimes rumbling. p. 108 CD 13-43

◀ **Timpani** Large, pot-shaped drums, also called kettle-drums. Unlike most drums, timpani can be tuned to notes of the scale. The timpani's voice can sound like a loud boom, a quiet thump, or a distant rumble. p. 274 CD 13-44

◀ **Trombone** A brass instrument with a large bell at one end of the tubing and a long, curved slide. The trombone can be loud and brilliant, but its soft voice is mellow. p. 185 CD 13-45

◀ **Trumpet** A brass instrument with a bell at one end of its coiled tubing. The trumpet's voice can be loud and bright, but can also sound warm and sweet. p. 185 CD 13-46

Instrument Key: strings percussion woodwind brass

Tuba A large brass instrument with a wide bell at one end of coiled tubing. The tuba's low notes are soft and dark-sounding. The higher ones are full and warm. p. 182 CD 13-47

Vibraphone A keyboard of metal bars played with mallets. Resonating tubes hang below each bar. A metal fan moves air through the tubes to create a vibrating sound. p. 147 CD 13-48

Viola [vee-OH-luh] A wooden string instrument that looks like a large violin. The viola is either bowed or plucked. The sound of the viola is deeper, richer, and darker than that of the violin. p. 109 CD 13-49

Violin A small, wooden string instrument that is held under the player's chin. The violin plays sounds from low to very high. A good player can create many unusual and interesting sounds on the violin. p. 109 CD 13-50

Xylophone A keyboard of wooden bars played with mallets. The xylophone has a bright, brittle sound. p. 144 CD 13-51

Sound Bank

Most instruments appear on the page indicated. In a few instances, the reference is to a family of instruments.

Glossary

AB form A musical plan that has two different parts, or sections. p. 18

ABA form A musical plan that has three sections. The first and last sections are the same. The middle section is different. p. 130

accent An accent is used to give emphasis to a single note. p. 205

accompaniment A part, usually played by one or more instruments, that supports a main melody. p. 32

arco Playing a string instrument with the bow. p. 109

ballad A song that tells a story. p. 344

bar lines The up and down lines in a piece of music that show how beats are grouped together. p. 127

beat The regular pulse felt in most music. p. 10

bordun A repeated pattern used to accompany music. It has two pitches, one of which is the home tone. p. 407

call and response A form of choral singing. The call is sung by a leader. The response is usually sung by a group. p. 54

canon A follow-the-leader process in which all perform the same pattern, but start at different times. p. 186

chord A group of three or more pitches sounding at the same time. p. 223

coda Music that ends a song after the words are sung. p. 134

countermelody A different melody that is played or sung at the same time as the main melody. p. 404

crescendo A sign that tells you to get louder. p. 196

D.C. al Fine A Italian musical term that tells you to go back to the beginning of the song and repeat until the word *Fine*.

decrescendo A sign that tells you to get softer. p. 196

double bar The up and down double lines that mark the end of a song. p. 127

downbeat The beat that begins a measure. p. 203

dynamics The louds and softs in music. p. 6

form The overall plan of a piece of music. p. 18

harmony Two or more different pitches sounding at the same time. p. 221

improvise To make up music as it is being performed. p. 115

introduction Music that is played before the words are sung. p. 134

legato Smooth and connected sounds. p. 83

measure The space between two bar lines. p. 127

melodic ostinato A melody pattern that repeats several times. p. 111

melody A line of single tones that move up, down, or repeat. p. 20

meter The way beats of music are grouped, often in sets of two or three. p. 165

octave The distance between one note and the next higher or lower note that has the same name. p. 139

ostinato A repeated rhythm or melody pattern. p. 37

partner songs Two or more different songs that can be sung at the same time to create harmony. p. 148

pentatonic Songs that have only five pitches. p. 26

phrase A musical sentence. p. 16

pizzicato Plucking the strings of an instrument with the fingers. p. 109

refrain A song part that is sung the same way every time it repeats. p. 93

repeated pitches Two or more pitches in a row that are the same. p. 61

rests Symbols for silences in music. p. 12

rhythm A pattern of long and short sounds and silences. p. 10

rondo A musical form in which the A section repeats between two or more contrasting sections. p. 207

scat A style of jazz singing where nonsense syllables take the place of words. p. 154

skip Moving from one pitch to another, skipping the pitches in between. p. 60

staccato Short and separated sounds. p. 83

step A move from one pitch to another without skipping a pitch. p. 60

strong beat The first beat in a measure. p. 124

style The special sound that is created when musical elements such as rhythm, timbre, and expression are combined. p. 40

subito A sudden change. p. 121

syncopation A rhythm where the note that is stressed comes between two beats. p. 51

tempo The speed of the beat. p. 46

texture How thin or thick music sounds. It is created by layering sounds on top of each other. p. 75

tie A musical symbol that joins two notes together to create a longer rhythm. p. 49

timbre The special sound each voice or instrument makes. p. 69

tonal center The home tone of a song. p. 211

unison When all instruments or voices play or sing the same notes. p. 109

upbeat One or more notes before the first strong beat of a phrase. p. 129

verse A song part where the melody stays the same when it repeats, but the lyrics change. p. 93

Classified Index

Poems and Stories

Recorded Interviews

Index of Songs

Song Index

Credits

Cover Photography: Jade Albert for Scott Foresman

Cover Design: Steven Curtis Design, Inc.

Unit Introductions: Steven Curtis Design, Inc.

Photograph Credits

viii: Archivo Iconografica, S.A./Corbis 1: Osamu Honda/AP/Wide World 1: Everett Collection, Inc. 4: M. & E. Bernheim/Woodfin Camp & Associates 4: M. & E. Bernheim/Woodfin Camp & Associates 4: © Tony Freeman/PhotoEdit 4: © Tony Freeman/PhotoEdit 4: PhotoDisc 5: Daemmrich Photography 5: Daemmrich Photography 5: International Stock 5: © Lindsay Hebberd/Woodfin Camp & Associates 5: © Lindsay Hebberd/Woodfin Camp & Associates 5: Paul Thompson/International Stock 6: *c* Everett Collection, Inc. 8: *tr* Everett Collection, Inc. 9: *cr* Everett Collection, Inc. 23: *bl* Archivo Iconografica, S.A./Corbis 30: *b* Liaison Agency 30: *tc* Liaison Agency 32: PhotoDisc 33: PhotoDisc 34: *cl* Osamu Honda/AP/Wide World 35: *bl* Brian Hennessey/Sony Classical 35: *br* Brian Hennessey/Sony Classical 40: © Daniel Lainé/Corbis 40: © Daniel Lainé/Corbis 40: Theresa Smith 41: *c* SuperStock 41: *c* SuperStock 42: Theresa Smith 43: *b* SuperStock 52: © Joe Viesti/Viesti Collection, Inc. 53: © Joe Viesti/Viesti Collection, Inc. 63: *c* © Neal Preston/Corbis 66: *bl* Werner Forman Archive/The Bradford Coll., Plains Indian Museum, BBHC, Cody, Wyoming, USA/Art Resource, NY 66: *c* ©Richard A. Cooke/Corbis 68: PhotoDisc 69: PhotoDisc 70: *c* R. Brandon/Alaska Stock 70: *cr* R. Brandon/Alaska Stock 70: *bc* Dorling Kindersley 71: Tom Chapin *tr* Nancy Brown/Singer/Songwriter Tom Chapin 71: *c* © Dorling Kindersley 71: *bl* © Dorling Kindersley 72: *bkgd* Richard Hamilton Smith/Corbis 78: *bl* © Bettmann/Corbis 78: *cr* Frances Kaplan Moore 78: *bc* Tom Raymond/Stone 78: *br* Charles Peterson/Archive Photos 78: *t* © D. Roundtree/Image Bank 78: *bkgd* PhotoDisc 79: *b* Metronome/Archive Photos 79: *cr* © Dan Scafidi/Drum Corps International 79: *c* Drum Corps International 85: *tc* Scala/Art Resource, NY 85: *bc* Christie's, London/SuperStock 85: *br* Christie's, London/SuperStock 85: William Johnson/Stock Boston 100: *bl* Asian Composers' League 101: *tr* Li Mei-Shu Foundation 108: PhotoDisc 109: PhotoDisc 110: PhotoDisc 113: *cl* Photofest 128: *bkgd* SuperStock 132: *bc* Vctoria & Albert Museum, London/Art Resource, NY 133: *cr* ©Jack Vartoogian 141: *c* Bettmann/Corbis 144: *b* Musser Company, a division of Ludwig 145: *bc* ©Gavin Smith/FSP/Gamma/Liaison Agency 146: *bc* ©Jack Vartoogian 146: *tr* PhotoDisc 147: *bc* ©Bertrano LaForet/Liaison Agency 147: *br* Musser Company, a division of Ludwig 152: *bc* PhotoDisc 154: Carmelo Blandino 154: Carmelo Blandino 154: Carmelo Blandino 155: Metronome/archive Photos 162: *tr* Corbis 163: *tr* Hulton-Deutsch Collections/Corbis 163: *cl* Corbis 173: *r* Frederic Remington Art Museum, Ogdensburg, New York 180: *bl* Japanese Music Institute of America 180: *tr* A.S.K./Viesti Collection, Inc. 180: *br* Jack Vartoogian 180: *tl* David Young/Wolff/PhotoEdit 181: *bl* Jack Vartoogian 182: *l* PhotoDisc 182: *tl* PhotoDisc 182: *bl* PhotoDisc 185: *cl* Cylla von Tiedemann/ICM Artists, Ltd. 196: *c* © Jim Bush/Buffalo Philharmonic Orchestra 202: *tr* ASAP 202: Len Rue, Jr./Animals Animals/Earth Scenes 203: *br* ASAP 205: *tr* Jack Vartoogian 205: *tl* Gerard Del Vecchio/Stone 210: *b* © Ted Levin/Animals Animals/Earth Scenes 211: *bl* Eugene and Claire Thaw Collection, Fenimore Art Museum, Cooperstown, NY, U.S.A./John Bigelow Taylor Photo/Art Resource, NY 211: *br* Eugene and Claire Thaw Collection, Fenimore Art Museum, Cooperstown, NY, U.S.A./John Bigelow Taylor Photo/Art Resource, NY 230: @2000 John Running 230: Public Domain 231: ©Jack Vartoogian 231: Courtesy of Vanguard Records, a/Welk Music Group Company 232: *bkgd* © Ken Biggs/Stone 232: *c* Teri Bloom Photography, Inc. 232: Teri Bloom/Photography, Inc. 232: *bl* © Torleif Svensson/The Stock Market 232: @2000 John Running 232: © Torleif Svensson/The Stock Market 233: *b* @2000 John Running 233: *bkgd* © Ken Biggs/Stone 233: *tl* Bob Daemmrich/Daemmrich Photography UO/7 234: *f* © Ken Biggs/Stone 234: *t* PhotoDisc 234: *bkgd* © Ken Biggs/Stone 237: *bl* Globe Photos, Inc. 237: *bl* Drew/AP/Wide World 242: *tl* Brent Jones 243: *cr* Indianapolis Children's Choir 243: *bl* Indianapolis Children's Choir 244: *b* Norman Seeff Productions, Inc. 244: *cl* Teri Bloom Photography, Inc 245: *bl* Robert Brenner/PhotoEdit 245: *tr* Bettmann/Corbis 249: *cl* @2000 John Running 251: *b* Corbis 252: *bl* Dennis Grant/Rip Roar Music 252: *tr* Lowell Georgia/Corbis 259: *tr* Public Domain 260: *c* © George Gerster/Photo Researchers, Inc. 260: *b* ©Jack Vartoogian 261: *b* SuperStock 261: *t* © Benelux Press/Leo de Wys Photo Agency 262: Eyewire, Inc. 262: Eyewire, Inc. 263: © DK Picture Library 263: © DK Picture Library 263: © Dorling Kindersley 263: © Dorling Kindersley 263: © Dorling Kindersley 263: © Dorling Kindersley 263: © Dorling Kindersley 263: © Dorling Kindersley 264: *c* © Danny Lehman/Corbis 266: *br* Paul A. Souders/Corbis 267: *bl* Michael S. Yamashita/Corbis 267: *br* Paul A. Souders/Corbis 268: *bkgd* ©Jack Vartoogian 274: Migdoll 275: Migdoll 275: *tr* © Bettmann/Corbis 277: *tc* Ulrike Welsch 277: *t* Robert Fried Photography 277: *bc* Victor Englebert 280: *b* © Michael Macintyre 281: *bl* © Ivan Strasburg 281: *br* © Liba Taylor 281: *bc* © Liba Taylor 282: *bkgd* The Newark Museum/Art Resource, NY 283: *bkgd* Crispin Hughes/Hutchison Library 283: *t* Lawrence Migdale/Stone 283: *c* Pictorial Press 285: *tr* PhotoDisc 286: *bc* Courtesy of Vanguard Records, a/Welk Music Group Company 290: Ilene Robinette 290: Ilene Robinette 290: Ilene Robinette 290: Ilene Robinette 292: Ilene Robinette 293: *t* © Rick Poley/Visuals Unlimited 296: *tr* SuperStock 298: *c* McDuff Everton/Corbis 301: Joao Baptista Felga de Moraes *c* Cortesy Joao Baptista Felga de Moraes 302: *bl* Leo de Wys Photo Agency 302: George Ancona *tr* George Ancona 310: *c* Owen Franken/Corbis 311: George Marshall *br* Monica Maynard 314: © Gary Bartholomew/Corbis 314: TSS/NASA/The Stock Solution 314: TSS/NASA/The Stock Solution 316: ARC Science/The Stock Solution 316: ARC Science/The Stock Solution 322: *c* PhotoDisc 324: *c* ©Frank Wing/Liaison Agency 324: *bkgd* PhotoDisc 325: *c* © Francis G. Mayer/Corbis 342: *tl* © David Young-Wolff/PhotoEdit 342: Joel Spector 342: Spencer Grant/PhotoEdit 342: SuperStock 342 *tr* © Bonnie Kamin 343: © Bonnie Kamin 343: *tr* Spencer Grant/PhotoEdit 343: *b* © Myrleen Ferguson Cate/PhotoEdit 343: © Myrleen Ferguson Cate/PhotoEdit 343: © David Young-Wolff/PhotoEdit 343: *tl* SuperStock 348: *cl* © Erich Lessing/Art Resource, NY 349: *cl* The Granger Collection, New York 356: Illustration from ZOMO THE RABBIT, copyright © 1992 by Gerald McDermott/reprinted by permission of Harcourt, Inc. 362: © David Atlas 366: Franklin Hammond 369: *br* © 1996 Jeff Day 369: *t* © Fabian Falcon/Stock Boston 373: *tr* SuperStock 405: *br* Robert von Bahr 372: *tr* Tom & DeeAnn McCarthy/The Stock Market 373: Jose L. Pelaez Inc./The Stock Market 373: *tc* Ariel Skelley/The Stock Market 389: *tc* PhotoDisc 390: *tr* Eyewire, Inc. 392: *tr* Milt & Joan Mann/Cameramann International, Ltd. 392: *bl* Keyphotos/The Stock Market 392: *br* Milt & Joan Mann/Cameramann International, Ltd. 393: *bl* Milt & Joan Mann/Cameramann International, Ltd. 393: *tr* Keyphotos/The Stock Market 394: *tr* AP/Wide World 394: *bkgd* Corbis 395: *tr* AP/Wide World 396: *tr* UPI/Corbis 396: *bkgd* © Bettmann/Corbis 397: *r* © Bettmann/Corbis 398: *l* © Ron Watts/Corbis Every effort has been made to obtain permission for all photographs found in this book and to make full acknowledgement for their use. Omissions brought to our attention will be corrected in subsequent editions.

All other photos: Pearson Learning and Scott Foresman

Illustration Credits

Shelly Bartek: viii Jared Lee: viii Susan Swan: viii Stephanie Power: viii Lauren Uram: 1 Rusty Fletcher: 1 Christopher Corr: 1 Elizabeth Sayles: 2 Anthony Lewis: 3 Rusty Fletcher: 6–8 Jared Lee: 10–11 Bernard Adnet: 12–13 Karen Stormer Brooks: 14–15 Ruth Nagle: 16–17 Christine Mau: 18–19 Steven Mach: 20–22 Lauren Uram: 24 Georgia Cawley: 26 Joe Rogers: 27 Ilene Richard: 28–31 Leon Zernitsky: 36 Ruth Nagle: 38 Karen Stormer Brooks: 39 Steven Mach: 39 Theresa Smith: 40–42 Kathleen O'Malley: 44–48 Will Terry: 48 Francesco Santalucia: 50–51 Ruth Nagle: 55 Lindy Burnett: 56 Stephanie Power: 60 Stacey Schuett: 64 Ruth Nagle: 66–67 Russell Charpentier: 68–72 Dennis Hockerman: 74 Kathleen O'Malley: 76 Tiphanie Beeke: 83–84 Christopher Corr: 86 Jared Lee: 88 Scott Peck: 92–94 Georgia Cawley: 96 Anthony Carnabuci: 98–100 Richard Stergulz: 102 Karen Patkau: 104–105 Shelly Bartek: 106 Anthony Carnabuci: 107 Jody Wheeler: 112 Tiphanie Beeke: 114 Scott Peck: 115 Tiphanie Beeke: 115 Jerry Tiritilli: 116–118 Wayne Parmenter: 120–122 Susan Gaber: 124 Susan Gaber: 124 David Cunningham: 126 Ruth Nagle: 130–132 Lori Lohstoeter: 134 Susan Greenstein: 136 Scott Peck: 138–140 Higgins Bond: 142 Tony Nuccio: 144–147 Anthony Lewis: 148–149 Scott Peck: 152 Carmelo Blandino: 154–156 Roberta Arenson: 158 Kelly Hume: 158 Roberta Arenson: 160 Tony Nuccio: 163 Carolyn Croll: 164–165 Christopher Kean: 165 Annie Lunsford: 166–169 Kelly Hume: 166 Brad Teare: 170–172 Jennifer Hewitson: 174 Susan Swan: 176 Kelly Hume: 176 Susan Tolonen: 178 Lydia Taranovic: 186–187 Nancy Freeman: 188 Lydia Taranovic: 191 Mitchell Heinze: 192–194 Guy Porfirio: 197–199 Steve Snider: 201 Fahimeh Amiri: 204 Richard Stergulz: 212 Karen Pellaton: 214–217 Jill Meyerhoff: 220 Burgandy Beam: 222–224 Roberta Arenson: 226 Guy Porfirio: 228 John Manders: 230 Ed Parker: 230 Tony Caldwell: 230 Rob Dunlavey: 231 Donna Perrone: 231 Jon Conrad: 231 Franklin Hammond: 236 Darryl Ligasan: 238 Renee Daily: 240 Jon Conrad: 242–245 Claudia Hammer: 246–247 Melinda Levine: 252 Anthony Carnabuci: 254 John Manders: 256 Dan Durkin: 265 Winson Trang: 270 Sally Jo Vitsky: 276 Susan Tolonen: 278 Eileen Mueller Neill: 284–286 Gregg Thorkelson: 287 Wayne Parmenter: 288 Ilene Robinette: 290–292 Sally Jo Vitsky: 295 Tony Caldwell: 296 Guy Porfirio: 304 Susan Spellman: 306–308 Marjorie Muns: 318 Chi Chung: 320 Annie Lunsford: 324 Douglas Klauba: 326 Gerardo Suzan: 328 Darryl Ligasan: 330 Steven Mach: 332 Naomi Howland: 336–339 Joel Spector: 340–342 Gloria Calderon: 344 John Sandford: 346 Kelly Hume: 346 John Sandford: 347–348 Eileen Hine: 350–352 Franklin Hammond: 354 Kelly Hume: 356 Joseph Hammond: 358 Rob Dunlavey: 360–362 Kelly Hume: 360 Rob Dunlavey: 363 Miles Parnell: 364 Franklin Hammond: 366 Marion Eldridge: 370–373 Nora Koerber: 374 Judith Mitchell: 376 Donna Perrone: 382 Fred Willingham: 384 Melinda Levine: 386 George Crespo: 388 Paula Wendland: 390–391 Ed Parker: 400

Acknowledgments

Credit and appreciation are due publishers and copyright owners for use of the following: 2: "Hello to the World," (c) 2000 by Susan Katz. 4: "Hello to All the Children of the World", from *Wee Sing Around the World* by Pamela Conn Beall and Susan Hagen Nipp, copyright (c) 1994 by Pamela Conn Beall and Susan Hagen Nipp. Used by permission of Price Stern & Sloan, Inc., a division of Penguin Putnam 7: "Supercalifragilisticexpialidocious." Words and music by Richard M. Sherman and Robert B. Sherman. (c) 1963 Wonderland Music Company, Inc. All Rights Reserved. Reprinted by Permission. 10: "Name, Name, What's Your Name?" by Jim Solomon. Reprinted by permission. 12: "Frog in the Millpond" from *Sail Away* selected and edited by Elinor Locke, 1981. 14: "Ding, Dong, Diggidiggidong" from *Music for Children, Vol. 1* by Schott, English version adapted from Orff-Schulwerk by Margaret Murray. 15: Excerpt from "Cats" by Eleanor Farjeon. Reprinted by permission of Harold Ober Associates Incorporated. Copyright (c)1957 by Eleanor Farjeon. 26: "Ida Red" from *150 American Folk Songs to Sing Read and Play,* 1974. 28: "Mud," Lyrics from "Beavers in November" (poem) by Marilyn Singer. Reprinted with the permission of Atheneum Books for Young Readers, an imprint of Simon & Schuster Children's Publishing Division from Turtle in July by Marilyn Singer. Text copyright (c) 1989 31: "Grasshoppers" from *Joyful Noise Poems for Two Voices* by Paul Fleischman. 36: "La pulga de San José" ("The Flea Market of San José") (c) 1994 José-Luis Orozco, Spanish lyrics and English lyrics and musical arrangement. All rights reserved. Used by permission. (c) 1972, 1997, José-Luis Orozco, Spanish and English lyrics and musical arr 43: "Three Little Birds" by Bob Marley. Copyright (c) 1977 Fifty Six Hope Road Music Ltd./Odnil Music Ltd./Blue Mountain Music Ltd. (PRS) All rights for United States and Canada controlled and administered by Rykomusic (ASCAP). All rights reserved. Used by perm 50: "Mister Ram Goat-O" from *Brown Girl in The Ring* by Alan Lomax, J.D. Elder and Bess Lomax Hawes. Copyright (c) 1997 by Alan

424

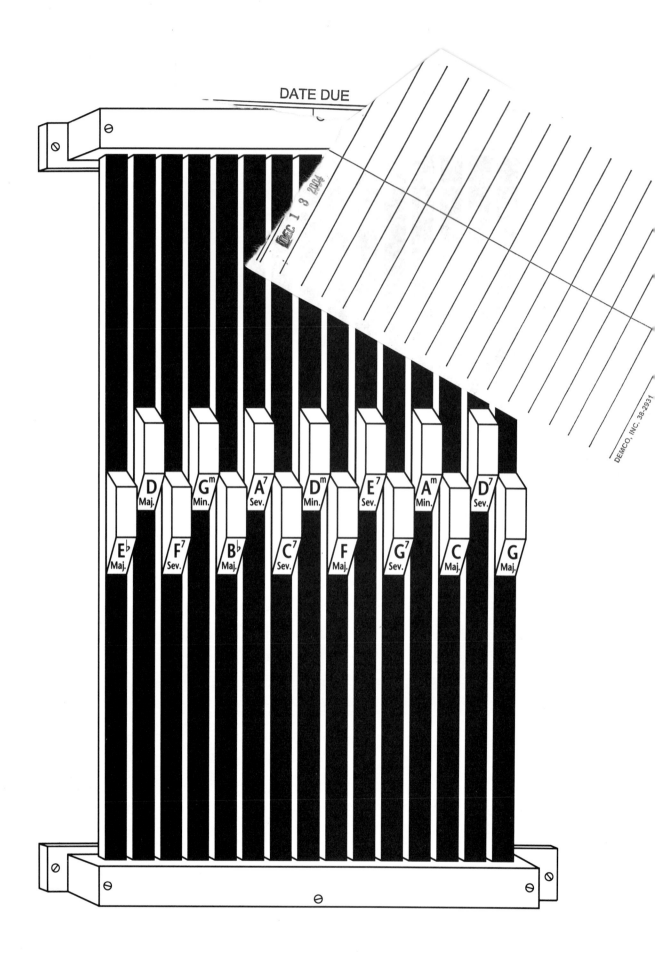